Who Made Early Christianity?

American Lectures on the History of Religions

This volume is the eighteenth to be published in the series of American Lectures on the History of Religions for which the American Council of Learned Societies, through its Committee on the History of Religions, assumed responsibility in 1936, and for which the American Academy of Religion assumed responsibility in 1995. Under the program the Committee from time to time enlists the services of scholars to lecture in colleges, universities, and seminaries on topics in need of expert elucidation. Subsequently, when possible and appropriate, the Committee arranges for the publication of the lectures. Other volumes in the series are Martin P. Nilsson, *Greek Popular Religion* (1940); Henri Frankfort, *Ancient Egyptian Religion* (1948); Wing-tsit Chan, *Religious Trends in Modern China* (1953); Joachim Wach, *The Comparative Study of Religions, Christianity* (1959); Robert Lawson Slater, *World Religions and World Community* (1963); Joseph M. Kitagawa, *Religion in Japanese History* (1966); Joseph L. Blau, *Modern Varieties of Judaism* (1966); Morton Smith, *Palestinian Parties and Politics That Shaped the Old Testament* (1971); Philip H. Ashby, *Modern Trends in Hinduism* (1974); Victor Turner and Edith Turner, *Image and Pilgrimage in Christian Culture* (1978); Annemarie Schimmel, *As Through a Veil: Mystical Poetry in Islam* (1982); Peter Brown, *The Body and Society: Men, Women, and Sexual Renunciation in Early Christianity* (1988); W. H. McLeod, *The Sikhs: History, Religion, and Society* (1989); Caroline Walker Bynum, *The Resurrection of the Body in Western Christianity, 200–1336* (1995); Wendy Doniger, *The Implied Spider* (1998); and Bruce B. Lawrence, *New Faiths, Old Fears: Muslims and Other Asian Immigrants in American Religious Life* (2002).

Who Made
Early Christianity?

THE
JEWISH LIVES
OF THE
APOSTLE
PAUL

JOHN G. GAGER

Columbia University Press
New York

Columbia University Press
Publishers Since 1893
New York   Chichester, West Sussex
cup.columbia.edu
Copyright © 2015 Columbia University Press

Library of Congress Cataloging-in-Publication Data
Gager, John G.
Who made early Christianity? : the Jewish lives of the Apostle Paul / John G. Gager.
pages cm. — (American lectures on the history of religions ; 18)
Includes bibliographical references and index.
ISBN 978-0-231-17404-6 (cloth : alk. paper) — ISBN 978-0-231-53937-1
(e-book)
1. Paul, the Apostle, Saint—Relations with Jews.   2. Identification (Religion)
3. Christianity and other religions—Judaism.   4. Judaism—Relations—Christianity.
5. Christianity—Origin.   I. Title.

BS2506.3.G34   2015
225.9'2—dc23

2014044886

∞

Columbia University Press books are printed on permanent
and durable acid-free paper.
This book is printed on paper with recycled content.
Printed in the United States of America

c 10 9 8 7 6 5 4 3 2 1
p 10 9 8 7 6 5 4 3 2 1

Cover Design: Jordan Wannemacher
Cover Image: Torah shrine. Courtesy of Yale University Art Gallery,
Dura Europos Collection.

CONTENTS

Acknowledgments   *vii*

INTRODUCTION   1

1. WAS THE APOSTLE TO THE GENTILES THE FATHER
OF CHRISTIAN ANTI-JUDAISM?   17

2. THE APOSTLE PAUL IN JEWISH EYES:
HERETIC OR HERO?   37

3. LET'S MEET DOWNTOWN IN THE SYNAGOGUE:
FOUR CASE STUDIES   53

4. TWO STORIES OF HOW EARLY CHRISTIANITY
CAME TO BE   87

5. TURNING THE WORLD UPSIDE DOWN:
AN ANCIENT JEWISH LIFE OF JESUS   117

6. EPILOGUE   139

Notes   *147*
Index   *185*

ACKNOWLEDGMENTS

T HESE chapters grew out of a series of lectures delivered in Atlanta, Georgia, in April of 2013. Sponsored by the American
Academy of Religion (AAR), the lectures form part of the series,
The American Lectures in the History of Religions. My lectures were delivered at Agnes Scott College, Georgia State University, Spelman College,
Morehouse College, and Emory University. My hosts for these lectures
were Jack Fitzmier, Executive Director of the AAR, and Lou Ruprecht of
Georgia State University. Without their friendship and constant support,
these lectures and chapters would not have happened. I am deeply grateful
to them. Their efforts went well beyond what was necessary. I must also
express my gratitude to the students from the various institutions who attended my lectures and raised important questions in our discussions.

The work reflected in these chapters reaches back over many years and
is indebted to many friends and colleagues in the Department of Religion
at Princeton. Martha Himmelfarb and Leora Batnitzky have shown en-
couragement at every stage of my work. Simi Chavel, Naphtali Meshel,
and Azzan Yadin-Israel (Rutgers) demonstrated outstanding patience and
knowledge as we worked through various versions of the Toledot Yeshu.
Peter Schäfer, my distinguished colleague for many years, served as both
mentor and helpful critic. He shared generously from his enormous knowledge of ancient Judaism. Michael Meerson has proved to be a reliable

resource at many points. Jeffrey Stout has been a constant companion. Undergraduate students, reaching back to 1968 at Princeton and elsewhere, have provided a constant source of inspiration.

This is also the place to recognize the work of my graduate students, who have become my teachers in this prolonged project. In the world of the academy, there can be no greater joy than seeing one's students flourish as distinguished scholars and teachers.

Two deceased scholars—Krister Stendahl and Lloyd Gaston—have exercised an enormous impact on my understanding of the apostle Paul. It is impossible to overstate what their work and friendship has meant to me over many years. I must also recognize the work of two Jewish scholars, neither of whom was known to me personally, whose work on Paul deserves far more attention than it has received—Jacob Taubes and Michael Wyschogrod.

I would be remiss not to acknowledge the support I have received from various Israeli colleagues, to whom I am grateful—David Satran, Guy Stroumsa, Israel Yuval, Hillel Newman, Maren Niehoff, Yair Furstenberg, and Yaacov Deutsch.

I must also acknowledge the two anonymous reviewers of my manuscript. They read it with great care and understanding. Their criticisms and suggestions aimed at making this a better book, not a different one. I can only hope that I have not disappointed them in following their proposals.

Some of the material in these chapters has appeared in earlier publications. Portions of chapter 1 appeared in my book *Reinventing Paul* (New York: Oxford University Press, 2000). Much of chapter 4 appeared in my essay "The Rehabilitation of Paul in Jewish Tradition," in *"The One Who Sews Bountifully": Essays in Honor of Stanley K. Stowers*, ed. C. Hodge, S. Olyan, D. Ullicci, and E. Wasserman (Providence: Brown University Press, 2013), 29–41. It is used here by permission. Portions of chapter 5 have appeared in various earlier publications, as indicated in the endnotes.

Finally, I dedicate this book to my beloved children—Kristin, Peter, and Andrea. They make living and working worthwhile.

Who Made Early Christianity?

INTRODUCTION

The vanquished have given their laws to the victors.
—SENECA, *ON SUPERSTITION*

SENECA, the aristocratic Roman philosopher, penned these words early in the first century CE. A variant of the saying was already in circulation in Rome; it expressed Roman anxiety over the pervasive Greek influence in every aspect of Roman life—art, architecture, mythology, philosophy, and more. Rome had defeated Greece on the battlefield but had been swamped by Greek culture at home.[1] Here Seneca deploys the saying to express his dismay at the spread of Judaism among Romans, a fact well illustrated by numerous Roman authors of the time. Jews had come to Rome as slaves in the first century BCE, but were now attracting Romans in disconcerting numbers. For us, the saying may serve as a useful reminder of Judaism's social and political status in the period that will concern us— from the fourth century CE to the modern era. Two points are essential: first, by the end of the first century CE, the vast majority of Jews lived in the Diaspora, outside of what the Romans had renamed Syria Palaestina; and second, from the time of Constantine (d. 337 CE), the first Christian emperor, onward, Rome was increasingly a Christian empire—he embraced the new faith around 312 CE and Theodosius I (d. 395 CE) adopted it as the official religion of the empire. Before that time, Jews and Christians had existed as religious minorities in the Mediterranean world, with Jews very much advantaged by virtue of their great antiquity. The cultural space that Christianity sought to occupy as it expanded beyond its Palestinian birthplace was already occupied by an older, well-established, and legally protected biblical faith. As shown in the following chapters, Jewish synagogues and their communities were prominent features on the cultural landscape of the Roman world and their demography included Gentiles as well as Jews. Jews in the Diaspora continued to occupy that space even after the crushing defeat of three successive anti-Roman revolts (66–73, 115–117, 132–135 CE), indeed after the time of Constantine and Theodosius. They presented a serious barrier to Christian efforts to establish themselves as the true biblical faith. That barrier would have to be removed or isolated if Christians were to create *their* identity as the true Israel and inherit the prestige and privileges of the Jews. The tools developed to dislodge these barriers were the rhetoric, and eventually the actions, of Christian anti-Judaism. But as shown below, these tools were never fully equal to the task and the barriers proved exceedingly difficult to dislodge.

Before the time of Constantine, and in some places long thereafter, Christians were newcomers and looked upon with deep suspicion. In the Roman world, Christianity was illegal. Numerous Christians, especially their leaders, were jailed, exiled, or put to death.[2] With the dramatic and unanticipated embrace of Christianity by Constantine and his successors, Jews, slowly at first, saw themselves vanquished yet again. In Roman law, Judaism remained a protected sect, but its space grew ever smaller. But here we must pause. The reversal of fortunes of Jews and Christians took place partly in the real world but even more in Christian rhetoric and imagination. This can be called the rhetoric of Christian triumphalism, with Judaism as the chief victim. The seeds of this triumphalism were planted long before the fourth century, but in Christian minds they came to full growth with the removal of Christianity's illegal status under Constantine and its adoption as the official religion of the empire several decades later under Theodosius. Three interconnected themes stood at the center of this rhetoric: Jews had been rejected by God and replaced by Christians as the true Israel, the new people of God; Christianity was the sole faith, the sole path to salvation for all humanity; as for Jews, there was no in-between—as

Ignatius had put it in the early second century, "If we still go on observing Judaism, we admit that we never received grace . . . It is monstrous to talk Jesus Christ and to live like a Jew."[3] In the rhetoric of Christian triumphalism, there was no space for Judaism. Jews no longer had anything to offer. Ignatius was the first Christian writer to put it such stark terms, but he will be followed by many others.

Placed side by side, the words of Seneca and Ignatius raise a number of interesting questions and point to a paradox. Why, if Ignatius is firmly convinced of Christianity's triumph, were some Christians still living like Jews? And what did it mean to live "like a Jew" (*ioudaïzein*)?[4] Ignatius does not say. Was there a crack in the armor of Ignatius's rhetoric? Did some Christians continue to live like Jews, not only in Ignatius's time but for decades and even centuries thereafter? As for Seneca, how is it that a vanquished people managed to impose their laws on the victors, that is, why were Romans being drawn to Judaism? Does this make sense? Beyond this, can we say that Jews imposed their laws, that is, their culture, on Christians as well?

The answer to this question is strongly affirmative. In virtually every corner of early Christian culture, Jewish influence makes its presence known: liturgy, holidays, theology, Christology, eschatology, communal life and leadership, ethics, Bible and biblical interpretation, art, and more. But the subject of Jewish influence is not the focus of this book. Rather we will look at the conditions that made such influence possible. What were relations like between Jews and Christians as the new faith moved into the heart of the Roman world? Did they conform to the rhetoric of Christian triumphalism? Did some Christians continue to live like Jews? What was it about Judaism that led Romans and Christians to want to live like Jews? How did Christian leaders deal with those who rejected Ignatius's all-or-nothing model, that you were either a Christian or a Jew but not both, and that Jews had nothing to offer? It will turn out that Jews had much to offer, not just to those on the margins but equally as much to those who placed themselves at the center.

Thus far I have spoken of Jews and Christians as if they were uniform groups. They were not. There were many types of both, often to the chagrin of their leaders. Among both groups, the multiplicity of groups led to harsh debates about who was the right group, the orthodox. Often Jews functioned in these debates as markers of the wrong groups, the heretics. Those who stood too close to Judaism were relegated to the margins, or beyond. Sometimes, those who lived like Jews were real people; at other times, they were convenient inventions. Christians who inhabited the borders or crossed them were seen as threats to the rhetoric of triumphalism. Leaders saw themselves as its guardians. Once again, Ignatius illustrates their role: "If anyone joins a schismatic, he will not inherit God's kingdom . . . Be careful, then, to observe a single Eucharist. For there is one flesh of our Lord, Jesus Christ, and one cup of his blood that makes us one, and one altar, just as there is one bishop."[5] Ignatius's heavy emphasis on unity and the authority of the bishop here is matched by, even born out of, his hatred of Judaism: "Now, if anyone preaches Judaism to you, pay no attention to him. For it is better to hear about Christianity from one of the circumcision than Judaism from a Gentile. If both, moreover, fail to talk about Jesus Christ, they are to me tombstones and graves of the dead."[6]

From this point on, I will emphasize the distinctive role of Christian leaders—bishops, theologians, abbots—as guardians both of Christian triumphalism and of its dangerous border-dwellers. One thing will become clear. It was leaders, those in positions of power, who stressed the absolute dichotomy of Christians and Jews. "Ordinary" believers, those not in power, the vast majority, frequently saw no need for such a division. This is an argument from social location. It is the distinctive role of those in power to stress unity and to patrol the borders. Others are free to move about, until they come too close to the borders and set off the alarms. Those who fail to heed the alarms become heretics. What all of this demonstrates is both the inherent fragility of Christian triumphalism and the perennial danger posed to it by the continued existence and flourishing of Jews and Judaism. And also by those Christians who chose to live like Jews. The result was Christian anti-Judaism, or in more abstract terms, conceptual nihilation ("they are to me tombstones and graves of the dead").[7] Dangerous threats must be eliminated, but as the history of relations between Jews and Christians will demonstrate, such efforts can never be successful. All ideologies are intrinsically unstable and in need of constant repair.

It should not be imagined that the process of conceptual nihilation was a one-way street, aimed only by Christians at Jews. From the very beginning, Jesus and his followers posed a threat to Judean leaders. It is no mere coincidence that the New Testament gospels identify Jesus's opponents as leaders of pre- and post-70 Judaism, the high priests of the Temple and the Pharisees. Whatever it was that they found unacceptable about the movement around the Jew Jesus, they were behaving like leaders. We need not believe that high priests and Pharisees *really* pursued Jesus throughout Galilee and Judea. These gospel stories surely reflect later conditions that have been read back into the time of Jesus. If we assume instead that these later conditions represent the time following the disastrous collapse of the revolt against Rome in 70 CE, we can well imagine that leaders who survived the defeat and emerged as Judaism's new leaders were not well inclined toward a small, schismatic group of Jews waiting for the end of history in the near future. They were dangerous, not just to these new leaders but to Rome as well. The repeated criticisms of Jesus reflected in the gospels—uncertain paternity, blasphemy, failure to fast, spirit-possessed, Sabbath-violation, insanity, magic—amount to conceptual nihilation: "The Pharisees went out and immediately conspired with the Herodians against him, how to destroy him" (Mk 3:6). Perhaps they did; in any case this is how the gospel writer saw things on the receiving end. But in this case too, it did not work. The movement survived and produced its own version of conceptual nihilation, Christian anti-Judaism. Jews did not remain silent. From that point on and through the succeeding centuries, the two will encounter each other in a recurrent cycle of attack and response. We will encounter another form of a Jewish effort to engage in conceptual nihilation in the final chapter of this book (chapter 5), when we examine the *Toledot Yeshu* (*Life of Jesus*). But it would be a serious mistake to imagine that Jews and Christians lived in a state of constant warfare. In many places and times they lived peacefully side by side.[8] But once the rhetoric of opposition was created and recorded, in written texts and oral stories, the potential for actual conflict was ever present.

In the early centuries of the Common Era, Christian anti-Judaism took primarily literary forms—records of debates between Jews and Christians, hostile stories, histories, and lengthy treatises.[9] At times, these words passed to deeds. This happened when Christians began to destroy synagogues, to convert them to churches, to expel Jews from their homelands, to kill them during the Crusades,[10] to murder them during the Inquisition, and, in its most gruesome culmination, to burn them in ovens. The common link between the words and the deeds is erasure. Some have sought to play down the intemperate rhetoric of figures like Ignatius, John Chrysostom, and many others. It is, they say, "mere" rhetoric; we should not take it too seriously, as if it expressed the true sentiments of the writers and speakers. The Jews in these texts are said to be "rhetorical" Jews. And it is said that the real audience of the words was an internal one, other Christians. I have no doubt that the immediate audience of Ignatius's letters, to cite but one example, was an internal Christian one. Fixed identities were being created and rigid lines being drawn. "Rhetorical" Jews were used to establish these identities. But to move from this observation to the claim that there were no "real" Jews in the world of Ignatius is a failure of logic. The issue is not rhetoric vs. reality, but the constant struggle to make the one fit together with the other. Judaism presented Christians with a real danger, not just to its rhetoric of triumphalism but to those pagans and Christians who continued to be attracted to synagogues.

The false dichotomy of rhetoric vs. reality crops up in other settings as well. The powerfully influential German historian Adolf von Harnack argued that with the rise of Christianity Judaism quickly retreated into self-imposed isolation and that Christians had no interest in Jews. Thus all of the literature, for example, in which Jews and Christians are portrayed as engaged in debate and discussion with each other must be read as pure inventions. There were no such debates, no discussions between Jews and Christians of any kind. It was all a rhetorical charade, using imaginary Jews to strengthen Christians internally and to convince their real, pagan audience of Christianity's antiquity and authenticity. For decades Harnack's view exercised a powerful effect on historians of early Christianity and Judaism. Today this view is untenable; it is anti-Judaism masquerading as scholarship. Marcel Simon was among the first to challenge Harnack. "Do men rage so persistently against a corpse?" he asked.[11] His counterargument, that Jews and Judaism remained entangled with Christians in multiple ways and that Judaism remained a lively and attractive religion for many centuries, will be a central theme of this book. From this perspective things look different. Debates did take place, sometimes in public[12] and sometimes in smaller circles.[13] Jews did meet Christians in numerous other settings—public baths, markets and shops, theaters and stadiums, business transactions, seminars and studies, and, as we will see in chapter 3, synagogues. This was true in Paul's time and it was still true three hundred years later.

I mentioned above that within the world of Christian triumphalism, Jews had nothing to offer to Christians. Christians had fully expropriated everything of value from the Jews—their name (Israel), their Bible (the Septuagint), their methods of exegesis (typology and allegory), their antiquity (by the claim to be the true Israel), their synagogues (which were converted to churches), and much of their postbiblical literature (Philo, the Jewish philosopher and exegete in first-century Alexandria, was so widely used that he was said to have become a Christian).[14] But here again, we find a crack in the rhetorical armor. Many Christians remained deeply engaged with Judaism and indebted to it. Three giants of early Christianity, each entangled with the other, are worth mentioning here: Origen, Jerome, and Augustine.

In several of his writings, Origen (d. ca. 250 CE) makes clear that he has consulted Jewish experts on a variety of questions.[15] In his commentary on the Song of Songs, written during his prolonged stay in Caesarea (Israel), he had been engaged in serious—perhaps scholarly—deliberations with Jewish experts on the meaning of the text.[16] On another occasion, when challenged by Christians, among them a certain Africanus, on his use of the disputed book of Susanna,[17] he justified his position by referring to conversations with a Jewish expert: "I remember hearing from a learned Hebrew, said among themselves to be the son of a wise man, and to have been specially trained to succeed his father, with whom I had conversations on many subjects."[18]

His massive undertaking in producing the *Hexapla*, containing six parallel columns of different versions of the Jewish Bible/Old Testament,[19] represents an enormous work of scholarship, but as he makes clear in his *Letter to Africanus*, what he had primarily in mind was to prepare Christians for discussions and debates with Jews about the meaning of biblical texts. Origen's interest in figuring out the correct version of the Jewish Bible was in no way a labor of disinterested scholarship:

> I make it my endeavor not to be ignorant of their various readings, lest *in my controversies with the Jews* I should quote to them what is not found in their copies, and that I may make some use of what is found there, even although it should not be in our Scriptures. For if we are so prepared for them in our discussions, they will not, as is their manner, scornfully laugh at Gentile believers for their ignorance of the true reading as they have them.[20]

In short, not only were such debates common in Origen's day, but he must have experienced claims by Jews that Christians misquoted biblical texts and cited passages that were not found in the best versions. From the very beginning, Christians had based their claims on biblical texts; Origen wanted to be sure that they got them right. Thus he appropriated Jewish expertise and used it to support Christian claims against the Jews.

To be sure, Origen describes the present condition of the Jews in sharply negative terms: "After the coming of Jesus, the Jews were altogether abandoned, and possess now none of what were considered their ancient glories."[21] Yes, he is a supersessionist, but of a very special, that is, Pauline, sort. In his lengthy commentary on Paul's letter to the Romans, he struggles to discover what Paul meant by three central assertions in Romans 11: First, what did the apostle mean in saying that "all Israel will be saved" (Rom 11:26)? Second, what is the point of his statement that Israel had stumbled but not fallen (Rom 11:11)? And third, how is it, for Paul, that Israel's disobedience (presumably to Paul's gospel) had led to the salvation of Gentiles (Rom 11:11–12)?

I believe that Origen follows Paul assiduously throughout and that he reaches the same conclusions: Israel's exclusion is temporary, not permanent; Israel's stumbling opened the way for Gentiles to reach salvation;[22]

and in the end, all Israel will be saved. Jeremy Cohen's observations on Origen's treatment of Paul are worth quoting at length:[23]

> Origen takes pains to delimit the extent of *carnal* Israel's rejection, making guardedly positive mention of the salutary character of the Jews and their role in God's historical plan . . . Jewish Israel stumbled temporarily but did not fall permanently. Its temporary lapse facilitated the salvation of the Gentiles.[24]

> Origen insists that their [the Jews] integration into the people of God remains a vital, indispensable component of the ultimate salvation.[25]

> This independence of the fate of the Gentiles and that of the Jews . . . embodies the "mystery" that Paul wished to unravel to his readers.[26]

> Origen does appear to assume that the Jewish people as a whole will regain their status as a community of God's faithful, that all Jews will eventually be saved.[27]

In the end, there are two serious differences between Origen and Paul. The first is the time scale. For Paul, the final resolution of Israel's status would come in his own lifetime, whereas for Origen that date lay in a distant and mythical future. The second concerns the conditions under which Israel would be saved. Cohen states that the Jews would be aroused "to believe in Christ."[28] In Romans 10:13, Paul quotes the biblical prophet Joel (2:32): "Everyone who calls on the name of the Lord shall be saved." For Paul, it would appear the Lord is God, whereas for Origen it is clear that the Lord is Jesus Christ (8:5). However that may be, here is Paul, in the middle of the third century CE, at the very heart of the debate about relations between Jews and Christians. Thanks to him, the issue was still unsettled.

The second great biblical scholar of the early centuries was Jerome (d. 420 CE). Although he lived almost two centuries later than Origen, and under a Christian emperor, his life was deeply embroiled with Origen and his legacy. Early in his adult life, Jerome had been an enthusiastic supporter of Origen; he had translated a number of his works into Latin and relied heavily on Origen's biblical commentaries in writing his own. But in later years, he turned against Origen and came to view him as something of a heretic. Jerome is best known today for his work in producing an authoritative Latin version of both testaments—the Vulgate.[29] He revised the older Latin versions of the New Testament and set about completely reworking the Latin Old Testament by returning to the Hebrew originals and providing new translations. From his monastery in Bethlehem, he sought assistance from Jewish scholars on various issues—to recover the original Hebrew of Jesus and his disciples, to learn the correct names of places, plants, and animals in the Hebrew text, to determine the accurate text of the Bible (on the assumption that false passages had crept into the Latin and Greek translations), and to ascertain the meaning of certain Hebrew words. Where the Hebrew differed from later translations, the Hebrew text carried the day. This is what Jerome called the *hebraica veritas*. While he was fully supersessionist with regard to Judaism and condemned Jews for misunderstanding and sometimes deliberately obfuscating their own scriptures (they remained at the historical or fleshly level and failed to understand the deeper spiritual, that is, Christian, meanings), they could be useful in getting things right at that lower level.[30] Especially since Jerome's knowledge of Hebrew was far from perfect.

As with Origen, Jerome's use of Jewish experts got him into trouble. His critics complained that he was giving too much credit to Jewish authority. Rufinus, the translator and defender of Origen, was one of these critics. Jerome had been taken captive by the Jews; he had become a *iudaicus spiritus*. Jerome, obstinate as ever, refused to back down. His goal, he insisted, was to recover the true text, which had been lost in Jewish translations and obscured by Jewish interpretations. And his experts were teachers, not masters.[31]

With Jerome and Rufinus we come to the third exception to the rule that Christians had nothing to learn from Jews—Augustine of Hippo. In a series of letters between Jerome and Augustine, the bishop of Hippo questioned Jerome on the need for a new translation of the Old Testament based on the Hebrew. For Augustine, the Greek Septuagint version was a sufficient authority; Jerome's translation threatened to undermine episcopal authority by changing the accepted versions and relying on Jewish witnesses. The second issue concerned Jerome's view that the dispute between Peter and Paul, as reported in the apostle's letter to the Galatians, was a staged controversy created to show Judaizing believers that Jewish practices were of no value.[32] Augustine's response to Jerome took an unexpected turn. Peter and Paul could not have told lies. Moreover, they were fully justified in observing the Jewish Law. Peter's only error lay in seeking to impose the Law on Gentile believers. Paul's only quarrel with Peter was on this issue; Peter should not have required Gentile believers to become observers of the Law. If this is so, Jerome thunders, what is to prevent Christians in Jerome's day from following their example and becoming Judaizers?[33] To Jerome's dismay, Augustine's reply went even further. Quoting 1 Corinthians 9:20 ("To the Jews I became a Jew"), he adds,

> *Paul was indeed a Jew*; and when he had become a Christian, he had not abandoned those Jewish sacraments which that people had received in the right way and for a certain appointed time. Therefore, although he was an apostle of Christ, he took part in observing these; but with this view, that he might show that they were in no wise hurtful to those who, even after they had believed in Christ, desired to retain the ceremonies which by the law they had learned from their fathers; provided only that they did not build on these their hope of salvation, since the salvation which was foreshadowed in these has now been brought in by the Lord Jesus.[34]

This was more than Jerome could take. Augustine had sold out to the Jews. In his letter 112, he erupted in a lengthy diatribe against Augustine and spelled out the dire consequences of his stance. What interests me here is Augustine's passing comment about "those Jewish sacraments which that people (Israel) had received in the right way and for a certain appointed time." Here he gives muted expression to a view that he will develop more fully in other writings, to the effect that ancient Israel was right to observe the Mosaic Law, that the Law itself was good and remains so for Jews, and that the continued existence of the Jews was essential to Christianity, for they guaranteed the authenticity of the biblical prophecies that pointed to the unique truth of Christianity.[35] Far from persecuting Jews, Christians must protect them. The proof lies in Psalms 59:11: "Do not kill them." This did not make Augustine a friend of "real" Jews. His Jews were mostly imagined or biblical. Like Origen and Jerome, Augustine was a supersessionist.[36] But Jews had much to offer and had to be protected. They were essential to the truth of Christianity. More than three hundred years after his death, Paul stood at the center of a raging debate.

Intriguing as these stories are in themselves, they reveal the fluid dimensions, the instability, the varieties of Christian supersessionism. To be sure, Christianity represented the sole truth; Judaism was overcome, rejected, and replaced. But the precise lines between Jews and Christians and between the two faiths remained worryingly uncertain. Rufinus wanted them to be watertight. For him, Jerome's use of Jewish experts was unacceptable. Jerome himself expressed concern over his use of Jewish experts (perhaps to defend himself against Rufinus's accusations) but nonetheless insisted on their value, even while criticizing Jewish translations and interpretations. And he was livid over Augustine's view of Paul as a Jew. This was Judaizing. Augustine in turn was nervous about Jerome's new, Hebrew-based translations of the Old Testament; there was no need to make use of Jewish experts. That threatened episcopal authority. But the Jews as a people, and their ancient scriptures, were indispensable to establishing the truth of the Christian faith. They must be preserved and protected.

By now, it will be apparent that a single thread runs through the entire story—the figure of Paul, the maker of Christianity. There were other threads, of course, but none like the figure of Paul. I sometimes worry that this may reflect nothing more than my own obsession. But a case can be made, though it requires careful restrictions. One way to state the issue is to ask this question: did Paul really make early Christianity? Of course not. Put in these simple terms, this is an impossible, unanswerable question. Not only did Paul not make early Christianity, he had no conception of what we call Christianity (chapter 1). As Augustine and others well knew, he was a Jew, and as many Jewish readers of Paul have understood, his goal was to bring Gentile believers in Jesus Christ into the eschatological people of God, not to annul the Law for Jews (chapter 2). Moreover, he expected the End to come in his lifetime. What we call Christianity is not just post-Pauline; it is un-Pauline. But for Origen, Jerome, and Augustine, he was and remained the maker of Christianity.

His name and his letters outlived his death and the failure of his expectation of the End. Paradoxically, the ecclesiastical groups, primarily in Rome and Alexandria, that came to shape the Christian scriptures, the New Testament, made him the founder of Christianity. His writings—along with others written in his name (Colossians, Ephesians, 1–2 Timothy, Titus), attributed to him (Hebrews), and written about him (Acts)—make up over 50 percent of the New Testament; two others (James and Mark) seem to have him in mind. Thus, if the New Testament represents the view in the third to the fifth centuries of where Christianity came from, the answer must be Paul. How could this have happened? After all, Paul had been a ruthless persecutor of the early believers. He fought Peter face to face in Antioch and called him a hypocrite. He expected the End in his own lifetime. In 2 Peter it is written that "there are things in Paul's letter that are hard to understand, which the ignorant and unstable twist to their destruction, as they do the other scriptures" (3:16). Paul himself complains constantly that his own communities have misunderstood him. In the second and third centuries he seems to have been most influential among groups—Marcion and "Gnostics" primary among them—who later came to be viewed as arch-heretics. So much so that Tertullian, the late-second-century heresy-hunter and promulgator of Christian orthodoxy, could call him—ironically, of course—"the apostle of the heretics." Tertullian is perhaps closer to the truth than he realized. Adolf von Harnack famously proclaimed that Marcion was the first Christian to understand Paul, though he misunderstood him. Robert Grant, writing of Paul's image in Marcion and Valentinus, two of emerging orthodoxy's arch-heretics, both of whom claimed Paul as their primary authority, concluded that "it is not so easy to prove them wrong."[37] In these early centuries, as Wayne Meeks observed, "the enemies of Paul were much less of a problem . . . than were some of his friends."[38]

So if it was not the "heretical" Paul who made early Christianity, which Paul did? What if we take another tack? Perhaps we can say that early Christianity gradually came to be as a result of its separation from its Jewish origins. Here we are on safer ground. The overall message of the church leaders who created the New Testament was separation from and triumph over Judaism. This is how they understood Paul. That was how his figure came to dominate the New Testament. He was the originator not just of the separation itself but of the harsh views that accompanied it— the views that must be labeled anti-Judaism. Here, remarkably, just about everyone agreed. Not quite everyone, but pretty close. Valentinus and his fellow "Gnostics," Marcion, Jewish Christians, mainstream Christians from Antiquity to the present, and nineteenth-century Jewish historians could agree on just one thing—Paul preached the need for all believers in Jesus Christ to separate themselves from Judaism; and he gave birth to the anti-Jewish theology of rejection-replacement. Jews had been rejected by God and replaced by Christianity. He converted to and simultaneously created Christianity. To be sure, in later versions of early Christian history, he was joined in these efforts by Peter. But in the early decades it was Paul alone. The Book of Acts states the case. Peter disappears once Paul appears on the scene. It is Paul alone who arrives in Rome. Peter is not in the picture.

This Paul, the father of Christian anti-Judaism, was enthroned as the maker of early Christianity. But not everyone thought that this was a good thing. Jewish Christians, who combined faith in Jesus with observance of the Jewish Law, accepted this image of Paul and for this very reason refused to call themselves Christians. Christianity without the Law of Moses was no faith at all and they wanted no part of it. It was a false religion, untrue to Jesus. And Paul was its creator. Some early Jewish critics of Christianity held a divided view. Paul did preach the need for Christians to separate from Jews, but he did not combine this with anti-Judaism. Not only was he not anti-Jewish, he was an emissary of the Jewish sages who sent him to preach a false gospel and to create Christianity as a fake religion. This is the view of Paul in several versions of the *Toledot Yeshu* (chapter 5). Today, among many Christian and Jewish readers, Paul is widely seen as a Jew whose mission was to bring Gentiles into the eschatological people of God at the end of history; anti-Judaism began not with him but with later "followers" who misread him by imposing their views on his letters (chapters 1 and 2).

So, which Paul created which Christianity? From the historian's point of view this is a silly question. No one person created Christianity and there never was a single entity called Christianity—or Paul. Diversity and dispute were the rule from the beginning and remain so today. There were many Pauls. But in a remarkable number of epochs, this is how he came to be seen—as the founder of Christianity. For some, this was a good thing; for others, not at all.

The making of early Christianity involved the drawing of lines and the defining of boundaries. Much of this work focused on Jews and Judaism. Of course, there were also concerns about pagans and paganism. But Judaism was a special case. Four factors guaranteed that this work could never be accomplished: the continued flourishing of Jewish communities and the lasting appeal of synagogues for many Christians (chapter 3); the existence of Jewish Christians, who combined faith in Jesus with Jewish observances and claimed that they alone embodied the true faith (chapter 2); Jewish critics of Christianity; and, most important, if least visible, of all, the memory that "we" were once Jews.

1

WAS THE APOSTLE TO THE GENTILES THE FATHER OF CHRISTIAN ANTI-JUDAISM?

It was Paul who delivered the Christian religion from Judaism . . .
It was he who confidently regarded the Gospel as a new force abolishing the
religion of the Law.

—ADOLF HARNACK, *WHAT IS CHRISTIANITY?*

FEW figures in Western history have been the subject of greater controversy than Saint Paul. Few have caused more dissension and hatred. None has suffered more misunderstanding at the hands of both friends and enemies. None has produced more animosity between Jews and Christians.[1]

We know more about Paul—by far—than about any other figure in the first 150 years of the early Jesus-movement. And yet there remains a host of unanswered questions. One of these questions is how this hugely controversial figure wound up at the very center of the New Testament, where, of the twenty-seven writings, more than one-half are either by him or attributed to him or about him. How did the "apostle of the heretics" become the heart and soul of the Christian Bible?[2] How did this zealous Pharisee, who by his own admission had been an active persecutor of the early Jesus-movement, suddenly emerge as a fervent follower of the risen Christ? How are we to understand his role as the apostle to the Gentiles, for this is how he always refers to himself? Should we think of this dramatic transformation as a religious conversion? If so, from what to what? Did he, for example, turn his back on his former life as a Jew and become the spokesman, even the creator, of early Christian anti-Judaism?

Not surprisingly, given his enormous impact on later Christian history, it has proved exceedingly difficult to pin down the "real" Paul. Only one set of issues has yielded anything like a lasting consensus. Lloyd Gaston has written that "it is Paul who has provided the theoretical structure for Christian anti-Judaism from Marcion through Luther and F. C. Baur down to Bultmann."[3] In short, Paul was the father of Christian anti-Judaism. And, I should add, for Harnack and many others this was a good thing! For them, Judaism had in fact been abandoned both by God and by history, because it was, in a word, a bad religion. And it had been replaced by a good religion, the only true faith—Christianity.

A brief outline of the traditional view of Paul as the father of anti-Judaism would look like this:

- Paul was a convert from Judaism to Christianity.
- His role as apostle to the Gentiles caused him to turn against his former life as a Jew.
- Underlying his new calling as an apostle to the Gentiles lies his belief that the Jews, having turned their back on Jesus as their Messiah, have been rejected by God as a disobedient people and replaced by Christians as the new people of God.
- Paul thus stands as the father of Christian anti-Judaism, the theologian of the rejection-replacement view. He also stands as the true founder of Christianity. These two stances are intimately connected.
- Paul was installed at the center of the New Testament precisely because he, like the later Christian communities that shaped these Christian scriptures and produced the New Testament, shared the rejection-replacement view of Judaism.

- As a Christian apostle, he repudiated the Law of Moses, the Torah, not just for Gentiles but for Jews as well.
- All of this is clearly laid out in his letters.

Despite the reigning consensus on these issues, it has long been recognized that it contains major difficulties. On every one of the preceding statements, Paul's letters offer up totally contradictory evidence. To illustrate these contradictions, consider two sets of texts, drawn from his letters: one set (A) anti-Israel, or anti-circumcision, or anti-Law; the other (B) pro-Israel, pro-circumcision or pro-Law set.

A. THE ANTI-ISRAEL SET

"For all who rely on works of the Law (= Torah of Moses) are under a curse." (Gal 3:10)

"Now it is evident that no man is justified before God by the Law." (Gal 3:11)

"For neither circumcision counts for anything, nor uncircumcision, but a new creation." (Gal 6:15)

"For no human being will be justified in his sight by works of the Law, since through the Law comes knowledge of sin." (Rom 3:20)

"Israel who pursued righteousness which is based on the Law did not succeed in fulfilling that Law." (Rom 9:31)

"As regards the gospel, they are enemies of God, for your sake." (Rom 9:31)

"But their minds were hardened; for to this day, when they read the old covenant, that same veil remains unlifted, because only through Christ is it taken away. Yes, to this day, whenever Moses is read a veil lies over their mind; but when a man turns to the Lord the veil is removed." (2 Cor 3:14–15)

B. THE PRO-ISRAEL SET

"What is the advantage of the Jew? Or what is the value of circumcision? Much in every way." (Rom 3:1)

"Do we overthrow the Law through faith? By no means. On the contrary, we uphold the Law." (Rom 3:31)

"What shall we say? That the Law is sin? By no means." (Rom 7:7)

"Thus the Law is holy, and the commandment is holy and just and good." (Rom 7:12)

"To the Israelites belong the sonship, the glory, the covenants, the giving of the Law, worship in the Temple, and the promises. To them belong the patriarchs and of their race, according to the flesh, is the Christ/Messiah." (Rom 9:4)

"Has God rejected his people? By no means." (Rom 11:1)

"All Israel will be saved." (Rom 11:26)

"Is the Law then against the promises of God. Certainly not!" (Gal 3:21)

Now the problem emerges. Point by point, the two sets contradict each other:

Circumcision is of great value; *it counts for nothing.*

The Law is holy; *it places its followers under a curse and cannot justify them before God.*

All Israel will be saved; *they are the enemies of God and have failed to fulfill their own Law.*

Here is a major dilemma for pious readers of Paul. No one wants an apostle riddled with contradictions. While many readers, including many New Testament scholars, simply ignore the problem, most fall into the category of what I call the "contradictionists," that is, those who recognize the tensions between the two sets of passages and set out to reconcile them. Among contradictionist readers, one finds four basic techniques for resolving these tensions—psychology, resignation, elimination, and subordination.

The psychological technique holds that Paul was lost in a hopeless quagmire of intellectual and emotional inconsistency. The converted ex-Pharisee sought to have it both ways. He had abandoned the Law and Judaism, but could not bring himself to admit it. He was simply unwilling to face the radical consequences of his new commitments, namely, that the Law really was obsolete, that circumcision really was of no value, and that being a Jew no longer counted for anything. The contradictory passages are thus assigned to opposite poles of his anguished psyche—the anti-Israel statements reflecting his "real" views as a Christian convert, the pro-Israel statements preserving his unresolved and yet-to-be-discarded loyalties as a Jew. Robert Hamerton-Kelly has written that Paul held on to Israel's role in the divine plan of salvation "due to personal factors" and "a case of nostalgia overcoming his judgment."[4]

The resigned technique simply leaves the contradictions as they stand, a position adopted by the Finnish scholar Heikki Räisänen.[5] Paul was simply incapable of straightforward, logical, consistent thinking. One consequence of this technique, and thus a significant handicap for many Christian readers, is that his thought is held to be of little theological value for Christians in their relations to Jews. Paul's thinking is such a muddle that it yields no useful guidelines for modern Christians.

By far the most radical technique is to remove the offending passages altogether. Typical of this approach is the Australian scholar J. C. O'Neill's treatment of Romans and Galatians. His basic view is that both of these letters were expanded and corrupted by later editors who profoundly misunderstood the apostle. Of Romans, O'Neill writes that its thought is "so obscure, so complicated, so disjointed, that it is hard to see how Paul could have exerted such an influence on his contemporaries if we assume that its preserved form represents his real thinking."[6] And so he proceeds to eliminate extensive passages on the grounds that they originated among post-Pauline, even un-Pauline, commentators: "If the choice lies between supposing that Paul was confused and contradictory and supposing that his text has been commented on and enlarged, I have no hesitation in choosing the second."[7]

The fourth technique, by far the most common, has been to subordinate the pro-Israel set, leaving the anti-Israel version as the true Paul. And for those who subscribe to the view of Paul as the father of Christian anti-Judaism, this means that the pro-Israel passages must somehow be explained away or just plain forgotten.

Until recently, few readers have bothered to consider an even more radical solution to these difficulties. Until recent times, few have entertained the possibility that the apparent inconsistencies of Paul's letters might be located not in him but in his later readers, in us. Why is it, I have often asked myself, that few have ever bothered—even as an experiment—to begin with the pro-Israel texts and to see whether the anti-Israel passages can be made to fit in? Put differently, almost no one has wondered whether it might be possible to construct a uniform and clear picture of Paul's teachings about the Law and Israel without convicting him of contradictory thinking, without subjecting his letters to radical excisions or pop psychology, while at the same time doing full justice to both sets of passages.

Following in the footsteps of Krister Stendahl and Lloyd Gaston, I argue here not only that such a picture is possible but that it is the only picture that makes sense of everything we know about Paul, his letters, and his times.[8] Beginning with the pro-Israel passages, I insist that Paul need not, indeed cannot, be read according to the contradictionists and that he is entirely innocent of all charges lodged against him by his anti-Jewish interpreters:

- He was not the father of Christian anti-Judaism.
- He was not the inventor of the rejection-replacement theory.
- He did not repudiate the Law of Moses for Israel.
- He did not argue that God had rejected Israel.
- His enemies and his audience were not Jews outside the Jesus-movement.
- He did not expect Jews to find their salvation through Jesus Christ.
- He was not a convert from Judaism . . . or to Christianity.

Obviously this will not be an easy task. Standing against me are not merely the obvious tensions between the two sets of texts but more than twenty centuries of reading Paul as the father of Christian anti-Judaism.

Standing with me are a number of recent readers, among them Jewish readers, who have set out to achieve the seemingly impossible—to reclaim Paul as a Jew and to reject the view of him as the father of Christian anti-Judaism.

WHERE DID WE GO WRONG?

By placing him at the heart of the New Testament, the churches established Paul—entirely against his own view of history—as the central figure in the subsequent history of Christianity and in its Bible, the New Testament. Entirely against his own expectations, he became *the* apostle, *the* supreme theological authority for every conceivable brand of Christianity, from then till now. But on one issue, virtually everyone agreed: he had rejected the Law and repudiated Israel. Of course there were exceptions. Jewish Christians, as we will see, took a different path. This made them heretics. And they took a negative view of Paul.

The dynamic at work here is a classic example of anachronistic reasoning. Since the recurrent message of the Christian communities that created the New Testament was the rejection-replacement view of Judaism, it stood to reason that Paul himself had to have been the spokesman, indeed, the originator of that view. From that time on, Christians and non-Christians alike have read Christian anti-Judaism back into Paul.

HOW CAN WE GO RIGHT? HOW CAN WE GO RIGHT?

Now I come to the hard part, where I try to show that this picture of the anti-Jewish, anti-Torah Paul is totally wrong and unjustified, from top to bottom. In recent decades, the tide has begun to turn against the old consensus. No longer is the traditional view taken for granted. Increasing numbers of Paul's readers not only question the old view but marvel that it ever came to be in the first place. A few citations will illustrate the new mood.

"It is nonsense to view the Pauline teaching of the Law . . . as an expression of the apostle's anti-Judaism."[9]

"How can people say that Paul teaches the divine rejection of Israel in chapter 9 when he expressly says the opposite in 11.1? . . . How has *Romans* 9 been turned into an anti-Jewish polemic?"[10]

"At least since the second century, readers of Paul have come to the texts assuming that God has rejected the Jews . . . I believe that Paul assumed just the opposite."[11]

"Paul nowhere suggests that the way to obedience for the Israelite lies in abandoning the Law."[12]

But still there are those pesky anti-Law passages. What are we to make of them, since it will not do just to ignore them? Where to begin?

Let me suggest that we begin by asking about the original settings in which Paul wrote his letters? Paul was not writing to the church of Saint Augustine in the fifth century, or to the Protestant Reformers of the sixteenth century, or to post-Holocaust Christians in the twentieth century. This sounds silly. Yet this anachronistic form of reading is precisely how the apostle to the Gentiles has been read throughout Christian history. He quickly became the apostle for all seasons. To be more precise, since orthodox Christianity persistently defined itself against Judaism, Christian readers have assumed that its great apostle must also have done the same thing. And the anti-Israel passages cited above seemed to establish their case. To cite one salient example, Tertullian, the polemical theologian of the late second century CE, wrote that "the primary epistle *against Judaism* is that addressed to the Galatians."[13] This is the setting in which Paul's letters have been read from the very beginning and the message is not Paul's.

My argument will be that a clear understanding of the concrete settings in which Paul wrote his letters becomes decisive in determining what they meant in their time. What were these settings?

The first setting concerns Jews and Judaism in the Roman world of the first century CE—the time of Paul. We now know that Judaism was a major religious and social force in the Greco-Roman world. Diaspora Jewish communities had existed in Mediterranean cities and towns for more than three hundred years before Paul began to preach his gospel to the Gentiles. Many non-Jews found the synagogue to be an open and welcoming place. All of this will be laid out in the succeeding chapters.

The second setting concerns the early Jesus-movement itself. It is clear that the Gentile-question—of what was to be the status of Gentile believers in the early Jesus-movement—roiled the early Jesus-movement. This question led to heated disagreements. The leaders of the movement (Peter, James, and Paul are those most commonly named) were bitterly divided. Some denied that Gentiles were admissible at all. Jesus addresses his followers with the words, "Go nowhere among the Gentiles and enter no town of the Samaritans. Go only to the lost sheep of the house of Israel" (Mt 10:5). Others held that Gentiles were admissible but only under certain conditions. They had to convert to Judaism, which, for males, meant being circumcised. This view appears in the words of anonymous believers in the Book of Acts: "Certain individuals came down from Judea and were teaching the brothers [= believers], 'Unless you are circumcised according to the custom of Moses, you cannot be saved'" (15:1). These are presumably the same people referred to in Acts 10:45 and 11:2 and Galatians 2:12 as the "circumcision party" (*hoi ek peritomês*). Their leaders are not named, but probably included Peter, and possibly James. These are the same believers who precipitated the struggle in Antioch between Peter and Paul. This is also the view of the gospel of Matthew. In chapter 5 of that gospel, Jesus presents himself as a hard-liner on observance of the Law: "Do not think that I have come to abolish the Law or the prophets . . . Unless your righteousness exceeds that of the scribes and Pharisees you will never enter the Kingdom of Heaven" (5:17–20). In this community, believers must have said, "Jesus was circumcised; we should do the same. Jesus affirmed and observed the Law; we should too." Yet another view held that Gentiles were to be accepted and admitted *as Gentiles*, without first embracing Judaism. No circumcision. This was Paul's preaching, but his position in this struggle was certainly the weakest. Was he really an apostle? Had he not sought to destroy the community of believers? "I was violently persecuting the *ekklesia of God and trying to destroy it*" (Gal 1:13). Not a promising beginning. His enemies must have thrown these inconvenient facts in his face at every opportunity. In fact, it is not too much to suppose that Paul lost out in this encounter at Antioch, for he leaves the city and never mentions it again.

We also know that the Law/Torah-observant party within the Jesus-movement not only insisted on circumcision for Gentile males but actively combated Paul and his Law-free gospel. What comes through, especially in his letters to the Galatians and to the Philippians, is that groups representing this view hounded Paul's efforts and followed him from city to city, preaching against his gospel and winning over members of his congregations to their point of view, that is, that circumcision was necessary for Gentile followers of Jesus. Here is the opening of his letter to the Galatians: "I am astonished that you are so quickly deserting the one [= Paul] who called you in the grace of Christ and are turning to another gospel . . . There is no other gospel . . . I place a curse on anyone who preaches a gospel contrary to what you received (that is, from me)" (1:6–9). To Paul's enraged dismay, those who were insisting on the circumcision of Gentile believers, the "circumcision party," had succeeded in winning over some (or all?) of the members of this community founded by Paul himself.

These are the enemies at whom he directs his anger and his arguments. *This* is the setting for his statements about the Law and circumcision— disputes entirely within the Jesus-movement, not with Jews outside. Galatians is a letter not against *Judaism* but rather against other apostles *within the Jesus-movement itself.*

Students of the early Jesus-movement have long known that these anti-Pauline leaders—*within the Jesus-movement*—followed him from town to town, seeking to impose their gospel of circumcision on his Gentile believers. The issue between Paul and his internal enemies was not whether Gentiles could become followers of Jesus. They could. The issue was whether they first had to become Jews—which for men meant undergoing circumcision—or whether, as Paul insisted, a new way for Gentile believers had been opened up by the faith and death of Jesus.

I must repeat here that all of this has long been understood by students of the early Jesus-movement. But only in the last fifty years have scholars slowly recognized that it is precisely these anti-Pauline apostles—*within the Jesus-movement*—who are the targets of his anger in Galatians and Philippians; it is against them that his arguments are directed. His negative statements about circumcision (Set A) have nothing to do with Jews outside the Jesus-movement. As the apostle to the Gentiles, he is focused exclusively on resisting the view that Gentiles within the Jesus-Movement had to be circumcised.

Now then, what happens to the traditional view of Paul, if we take *these* facts and *these* settings as starting points for reading his letters? First, it becomes clear that Paul's exclusive concern, as the apostle to the Gentiles, was the new status of Gentile believers, *not* the status of Israel. Gentile believers are saved, but not by becoming Jews. Thus when we read his letters we should always ask as our first question, how does this passage apply to his work with Gentiles? Second, we know that he was constantly on the defensive, not against Jews outside the movement but against his enemies within. The defense of his gospel preoccupies him throughout his letters to the Galatians and the Philippians, where his opponents must be seen as anti-Pauline apostles who were bent on undermining his gospel in any way possible; these people, within the Jesus-movement, are the targets of his anger and his arguments. Thus, his arguments against the validity of circumcision and the Mosaic covenant (Set A) apply only to the status of the Law for Gentiles within the Jesus-movement. They have no bearing whatsoever on their validity for Israel. For me, this merely confirms what he says explicitly in Romans, which is that the Mosaic covenant and circumcision remain fully valid for Israel.

To be sure, I must admit that virtually all subsequent interpreters have read him in just the opposite fashion. And if I am right, this misreading began already in his own lifetime; he complains repeatedly and bitterly that his followers had misunderstood him on all sorts of issues. But Paul himself is as clear as anyone can be that this was not his position: "Circumcision is indeed of value if you follow the Law" (Rom 2:25). And there is more. Paul never speaks of Gentiles (those living in the first century whom we mistakenly call Christians) as replacing Israel or of God as having rejected Israel in favor of a new chosen people. Once again, I cannot deny that virtually every subsequent interpreter has read him in just this way, but I must emphasize that Paul vehemently repudiates this misreading and seeks to correct it in his letter to the Romans: "I ask, then, has God rejected his people [Israel]? By no means!" (Rom 11:1). Finally, Paul never speaks of Israel's redemption in terms of Christ. Just as he no longer thinks of salvation for Gentiles within the Mosaic covenant, so he does not imagine salvation for Jews as happening through their acceptance of Christ.

WHAT IS WRONG WITH THE NEW VIEW?

These are the issues at the center of the reimagined Paul. What is wrong with it? What could one raise by way of objections. At a basic level, there is always resistance to change. And this change is not about something trivial. Christians—and Jews—have long been committed to the view of Paul as the father of Christian anti-Judaism. To throw that into doubt requires deep and sometimes painful revisions on the part of just about everyone. This new view destabilizes Judaism and Christianity at their very foundations. And there are other objections. Some have said that there is no such view of Paul to be found anywhere in later Christianity. If true, that would be serious. But it is not true. As we will see in chapter 4, the *Pseudo-Clementines*, a Christian text widely circulated in the second through the fifth centuries CE, advanced the view that Gentile Christians and Jews follow different paths, both equally authentic, one of Jesus, the other of Moses. Jewish Christians observed and defended the Law. The *Epistle of Barnabas* (from the late first or early second century) warns its readers against those who assert that "the covenant is both theirs and ours" (4.6).[14] And other Jewish authors long before the modern period argued that Paul had not rejected either the Law or Israel. They insisted that Christians had misunderstood their own scriptures.

Another objection has sometimes been raised, claiming that the idea of Gentile salvation or redemption without conversion is without precedent in Judaism. This too is false. There were, of course, Gentile proselytes, full converts; for Philo, as we will see, they had earned a special place of honor on the day of judgment. There were also "righteous Gentiles," which designated non-Jews who followed the so-called Noachide Laws or commandments,[15] a body of regulations developed within Judaism specifically for Gentiles and circulating as early as the late first century BCE. Such Gentiles could be called "righteous."[16] There were also "god-fearers," or friends of the synagogue who participated in various aspects of Jewish life. But our question is whether Gentiles who were not converts could be *saved* in the last days. What was the fate of eschatological Gentiles? E. P. Sanders and others have pointed out that Jews of the early centuries CE held no single view on this question. Among the rabbis, "different attitudes towards the Gentiles prevailed at different times."[17] For some, all Gentiles would be condemned. Others anticipated the final conversion of the Gentiles. Still others believed that righteous Gentiles would be saved, *as Gentiles*, at the End. The Tosefta, an early compilation of Rabbinic debates and decisions (from around 250 CE), records a dispute between R. Eliezer and R. Joshua. The dispute centers on a line from Psalm 9:17: "The wicked shall return to Sheol, all the heathen that forget God." R. Eliezer holds that "none of the heathen has any share in the world to come." R. Joshua replies: "If Scripture had said: 'The wicked shall return to Sheol, all the wicked,' and stopped there, I would have spoken according to your words; but since Scripture says: 'Who forget God,' behold there must be righteous men among the heathen *who have a share in the world to come*." Apart from these early rabbis (both were slightly older than Paul), there were other texts in wide circulation that envisaged a happy fate for righteous Gentiles, *as Gentiles*, at the End.[18] Paula Fredriksen puts it succinctly: "this 'turning' to Israel's god is not the same as converting to Judaism . . . the nations join *with* Israel, but they do not *join* Israel."[19] Paul says so explicitly in his first letter to the Thessalonians. He rejoices in the report that Gentile believers there had "turned to God from idols, to serve a living and true God, and to wait for his Son from heaven . . . Jesus, *who rescues us from the wrath that is coming*" (1:9).

When I first began to contemplate the possibility of an entirely new view of Paul—the view that he was not the father of Christian anti-Judaism, indeed that he was not Christian at all—I was guided by the work of powerful predecessors. Krister Stendahl's book *Paul Among Jews and Gentiles* (1976)[20] and Lloyd Gaston's essay "Paul and the Torah" (1977)[21] broke the mold. Stanley Stowers's *A Rereading of Romans: Justice, Jews, and Gentiles* (1994)[22] strengthened my resolve. I still remember the shock after reading Gaston. What was he demanding? Where did his conclusions leave us, not just believing Christians but all students of early Christianity? If he was right, pretty much everything went out the window. Gaston himself seems to have undergone something like a conversion experience: "I suddenly find that I have great difficulty in reading the standard literature on Paul: why do other interpreters miss the obvious while spending much time on matters not in the text at all. I find that I cannot trust such 'objective' works as lexica on some points. It's almost paralyzing when it comes to writing, for so little can be assumed and all must be discussed."[23] We have to start all over again, from the very beginning. But these scholars (Stendahl and Gaston) were Christians. Were they just post-Holocaust Christian apologists guilty of seeking to get the apostle off the hook as the source of Christian anti-Judaism, of anti-Semitism, and ultimately of the Holocaust? Gaston himself is open about what is at stake for him: "A Christian Church with an anti-Semitic New Testament is abominable, but a Christian Church without a New Testament is inconceivable . . . A New Testament without . . . the Pauline corpus as its formal center would not be the New Testament at all."[24]

What, I wondered, would Jewish readers make of this? Was this just too much? Could they possibly embrace this new view? Gradually, as I became familiar with Jewish readers who had in fact adopted the new view, I remained puzzled. Why would Jewish readers, of all people, set out to reclaim Paul, of all people? Was he not beyond redemption? Jews had long claimed that Jesus was a Jew. But among many Jews, Paul was the father of Christian anti-Judaism. How could he be redeemed? Here I need to make a confession. At first it made no sense to me. But slowly I came to a different view. Why not Jews? If Paul really was a Jew, if the framework for understanding him lies in first-century Judaism, who better than those who best understood that Judaism, *sine ira et studio*, without bitterness or partiality. Or as G. F. Moore put it in 1921, without apologetics or polemics.[25] There is much more to say about this revolutionary turn among Jewish readers;

I will return to them in the following chapters. Here, for reasons that will become obvious, I want to consider just one of these readers.

A JEWISH READER OF PAUL: JACOB TAUBES

Jacob Taubes was a German rabbi, a philosopher, a disciple of Gershom Scholem, and a professor at Princeton and Columbia. Eventually he returned to Germany and assumed a position in Berlin at the Free University. In 1987 he delivered a spell-binding series of lectures to a largely Protestant audience in Heidelberg, Germany. Advertised as a four-day course on Paul's Epistle to the Romans, the lectures were delivered, without notes, just weeks before his death from cancer.[26] Taubes spoke on Monday, Tuesday, Thursday, and Friday; he spent Wednesday in the intensive care unit of the local hospital. Well aware that the end was near, he cut to the chase. Time was short. No need for footnotes. The language of the lectures is direct and blunt, highly personal and full of humor.[27] Of himself, he confesses to his "uneasy Ahasueric lifestyle at the borderline between Jewish and Christian."[28] Not back and forth, but somewhere in between. In the same space, I would argue, occupied by Paul. "Now I of course," he said, "am a Paulinist, not a Christian, but a Paulinist."[29]

What drew Taubes to Paul? Part of the answer lies in his conviction—shared by other European philosophers (Agamben, Badiou, Žižek[30])—that Paul stands at the center of all modern philosophy and theology. For better or worse, Paul forms the core of Western civilization. Another reason for Taubes's obsession with Paul is clearly autobiographical. Taubes, like his version of Paul, dwelt on the borderline between Jewish and Christian. Not that Taubes ever embraced any form of Christianity, but rather that he felt at home in his Jewish version of Pauline "Judaism."

In one sense, Taubes's lectures belong with the work of other European philosophers who highlight what they called "Pauline universalism." But even more than that, he embraced their use of Paul's apocalyptic thought as the basis for a cultural and political critique of modern European (and, in

Taubes's case, American) culture. But unlike these openly a-religious think-ers, Taubes reads Paul as a Jew. He insists that he is able to understand what he calls the "Yiddish" of Paul's letters precisely because he is Jewish.[31] And while he is concerned to rescue Paul as a modern cultural critic, he does not dehistoricize him. Moreover he has done his homework. He delights in flaunting his knowledge of up-to-date New Testament scholarship, the thicker the better. And he chides his philosophical colleagues for their abysmal ignorance of the Bible.

That Taubes's Paul remained a Jew throughout his life cannot be doubted. He says so repeatedly:

> This is the point at which little Jacob Taubes comes along and enters into the business of gathering [*Heimholung*] the heretic back into the fold, be-cause I regard him—this may be my own personal business—as more Jew-ish than any Reform rabbi, or any Liberal rabbi I ever heard in Germany, England, America, Switzerland, or anywhere."[32]

> Paul is a fanatic! Paul is a zealot, a Jewish zealot.[33]

> I am inclined to assume that Paul was a Diaspora Jew . . . If he comes from the Galilean tradition, then it makes a lot of sense to me that he also calls himself a "zealot." And don't come telling me that as a technical term for the Zealots it comes up for the first time in Josephus.[34]

> The apostle takes the election of Israel seriously. This is embarrassing for modern Christianity, but that's the way it is. It's embarrassing. You've got to be able to live with this.[35]

In the end, Taubes leaves open the question raised by Romans 11:26 ("All Israel will be saved"): How will Israel be saved? Who will be Israel's savior? For him, the weight falls on Paul's goal in his immediate present, not on some imminent or distant future: "For Paul, the task at hand is the *establishment and legitimation of a new people of God*."[36] He is able to make this move because he measures Paul's apocalyptic time not in chronological units but in human, existential ones: "the Kingdom of God is not the *telos* of the historical dynamic; it cannot be set as a goal. From the standpoint of history it is not goal, but end."[37]

In sum, Paul remains a Jew because Taubes seeks, as one critic has put it, "to undermine the Christian image of Paul."[38] At the same time, Paul the Jew becomes the vehicle that enables Taubes to develop "a more sophisticated understanding of Judaism itself—one which sees Judaism as a phenomenon that has historically, from time to time, *demonstrated a tendency to seek liberation from the Law*."[39] Paul thus becomes the ultimate cultural critic. Here Taubes summons the monumental work of his mentor, Gershom Scholem, on the messianic figure of Sabbatai Zvi from the mid-1600s to show that Paul's effort to transvalue the Law must be seen as an authentically Jewish gesture.[40] This does not mean that Taubes in any way abandoned his Judaism. That would have made him undialectical, un-Pauline. It would have removed him from the ill-defined and uncomfortable world of Paul, "where what was 'Jewish' and what was 'Christian' had not yet been decided."[41] Yet it is more than that, for as Taubes argues, the word and the concept of 'Christian' had not even been invented:[42] "What is exciting in Paul is that we are *just before the turning point*."[43] And in an obvious swipe at New Testament scholars and Christian theologians, he insists that "the word 'Christian'—this I ask you to get into your heads—doesn't exist yet. One mustn't be cleverer than the author and impute to him concepts that he doesn't have and doesn't want to have."[44]

CONCLUSIONS, OR WHAT THE NEW VIEW TELLS US

By now it should be obvious that "new readers" are advocating a reading of Paul not simply as one possible alternative, as one contender alongside others, but as the only historically defensible reading. This is a bold stance. To some it will seem foolish. It is certainly out of step with modern theories that regard all views as possible. It is also highly presumptuous, even arrogant, in its insistence that twenty centuries and most readers of Paul have been mistaken and in demanding that they confront the sources of that mistake.

As a final note, a skeptical reader might well ask, "How can you (plural) claim that two thousand years of readers have misread Paul? Not just on matters of detail, but to the point of completely reversing his view of the Law and Israel!" In fact, anyone making such a claim must shoulder an enormous burden of proof. I take this to mean that we do not have the right simply to advance a new reading of Paul and that we must also offer an account of how the misreading came to be in the first place.

Proponents of the "new" Paul have not shirked this burden. W. D. Davies has put it this way: "Why letters specifically addressed to Gentiles should have come to be understood as opposing Judaism is not hard to explain." And he continues: "the loss of Paul's historical and cultural context . . . led to a different Paul." And he concludes: "when his letters came to be read by Gentiles who little understood Judaism, the misinterpretation became almost inevitable."[45]

The result is what one scholar has called a "domesticated apostle."[46] Another has written that "the price the Apostle had to pay to be allowed to remain in the church was the *complete surrender of his personality and historical particularity*."[47] Anachronistic readings have serious consequences. And they have proved stubbornly difficult to overturn. This is the task that has launched me on my quest for the Jewish lives of the apostle Paul.

While the "new Paul," or the "new perspective" as it has come to be called, has gained momentum in recent years, it has spawned numerous enthusiasts but also many doubters. The term itself carries many different meanings. For some, most notably E. P. Sanders, it means that New Testament scholars have profoundly misunderstood ancient Judaism and derived their views from a misreading of Paul. Paul never criticized Judaism. He simply held that a new religion (of Christ and Christianity) had replaced the old (of Judaism and the Law). For others, especially conservative and evangelical Protestants, the new view represents a threat to deeply held theological views and religious self-understanding. Ernst Käsemann, one of my former teachers and certainly no evangelical, drew these dire consequences from Krister Stendahl's essay "The Apostle Paul and the Introspective Conscience of the West (1963):[48] "It follows from this that Protestantism is no longer generally in accord with the Reformation any more. The scriptures have ceased to be accounted the basis and tribunal of the church . . . Practically speaking, the church takes precedence over the scriptures, even when this is not admitted in principle."[49] For Käsemann the stakes are extraordinarily high. If Stendahl and others are right, authentic Protestantism has lost its legitimacy. Most doubters argue that the new perspective has misread Paul: the break with Judaism came already with the new faith in Jesus; Paul simply followed that logic to the end.[50] And of course there are moderates of various stripes.[51]

Let me conclude with a personal anecdote. Several years ago, I delivered a lecture in Jerusalem on the "new Paul." Following the talk, an evangelical pastor spoke to me: "I love your view of Paul. I don't understand why my evangelical colleagues don't get it. What are they afraid of?"

2

THE APOSTLE PAUL
IN JEWISH EYES
Heretic or Hero?

In contrast to successful efforts to recover a Jewish Jesus, Jewish
scholarship has not been able to reclaim Paul.
—P. HAGNER, "PAUL IN MODERN JEWISH SCHOLARSHIP"

I N 1987, Jacob Taubes wrote that "the Jewish study of Paul is in a very sad state. There is a literary corpus about Jesus, a nice guy, about the rabbi in Galilee . . . *But when it comes to Paul, that's a borderline that's hard to cross*."[1] As seen in the previous chapter, Taubes stood out among Jewish readers of his day as someone who was prepared to reclaim Paul, not just as fully Jewish but as a Jew who offers the possibility of restoring both Judaism and Christianity to their authentic roots.[2] Yet, as I will argue below, Taubes's remark about the lack of Jewish attention to Paul does not tell the full story. A number of earlier Jewish writers have moved well beyond the notion that Paul rejected the Law and the Jewish people. Not just in recent decades, but many centuries ago.[3]

Let me begin by briefly recalling a few of the known facts about Paul's engagement with Jews in his own lifetime. In the first part of his life, he lived as a zealous Pharisee. At least in his own mind, he was a hero to himself: "I advanced in Judaism beyond many among my people of the same age, for I was far more zealous for the traditions of my ancestors" (Gal 1:14). At the very same time, he was a heretic, or worse, to the followers of Jesus. This is how he describes himself in this first part of his life: "I was violently persecuting the *ekklêsia* of God and trying to destroy it" (Gal 1:13). This is pretty powerful talk. Was it really that bad? Many Christian interpreters have tried to play down the note of violence. But the Book of Acts seems to reinforce Paul's rhetoric: "Saul was ravaging the *ekklêsia* by entering house after house; he was dragging off men and women and sending them to prison" (8:3); and in the story of Stephen's lynching by a Jewish mob in Acts 7 and 8, the last line states that "Saul (Paul) approved their killing of Stephen." Whatever the motivations for his violent persecutions of these Jesus-followers, there is no doubt that he saw them as violating central values of his Judaism and deserving of the supreme punishment.

But as we now know, something changed in Paul's life—something quite dramatic. This has sometimes been called a conversion—probably a misleading name, because it immediately suggests that he moved from one religion to another; far better is Krister Stendhal's choice of the term "calling." In calling himself "the apostle to the Gentiles/nations," Paul must have had in mind the prophet Jeremiah, who records that the word of the Lord had appointed him *a prophet to the nations* (1:5). So Saul, as he was then called, was summoned to be the apostle of Jesus Christ to the Gentiles. The result of this transformation was a complete reversal of his status as heretic and hero. As he puts it in his letter to the Philippians (Phil 3:7–8), everything was turned upside down. Once a persecutor of Jesus-believers, he became an equally passionate apostle. Now the picture gets complicated. For with this transformation, he became a heretic and a troublemaker among non-Jesus Jews. In the Book of Acts he is chased from one town to another for his disruptive preaching in local synagogues. Paul himself writes: "five times I have received from Jews the forty lashes minus one" (2 Cor 11:24–26), a biblical punishment (Deut 25:3) reserved for Jews who violated basic values and practices of the community.[4] The former Jewish hero had become a Jewish heretic. Among Christians he soon came to be regarded as the heroic father of Christian anti-Judaism.

Here a question arises: given this starting-point in the apostle's relations with other Jews, what reactions to him would we expect to find among Jews in later centuries? It seems fair to say that we would expect two responses: first, a hostile view of the apostle as the enemy of the Jews; and second, an unbroken line of diatribes against him in mainline Jewish literature—by this I mean primarily Rabbinic literature—from the second century to the present. In fact, we do find some of these reactions, *but only beginning in the nineteenth century.* The idea of a centuries-long, unbroken chain of anti-Pauline writings among Jews just doesn't exist. In all of Rabbinic literature there is not a single mention of Paul. It is only among Jewish historians at the dawn of the modern era that Paul emerges as a controversial target. The great German historian of the late nineteenth century Heinrich Graetz once insulted a personal enemy by charging that "since Paul of Tarsus, Judaism has not known such an enemy in its midst."[5] Somewhat later, in the first modern treatment by a Jewish scholar, Joseph Klausner wrote that Paul's negative view of the Law or Torah amounted to a "contradiction of the Jewish religion and a rejection of the Jewish people."[6] As a result, the apostle was rejected not only by Jews but by Jewish Christians as well. Klausner concluded with these words: "the fact has become clear that *the Jews could not have taken any attitude toward Paul except a negative one. So in his time, and so after his time, up to the present.*"[7] I could cite similar lines from other authors, but I will leave Graetz's and Klausner's words as a summary of what we might call the threefold Jewish view of Paul among modern Jewish scholars:

- The Jewish view of Paul has been consistently negative; he is the quintessential Jewish heretic.[8]
- Opposition to Paul has been constant, from the first century to the present.
- While many Jews have sought to reclaim Jesus as a pious Jew of the first century, no such rehabilitation is possible for Paul.

The motto sometimes heard is "Jesus, yes, but Paul, never."[9] Martin Buber offers a classic example of this view. For him, Jesus was a loyal Jew, fully in line with the Old Testament. But Paul, blinded by the light of his Greek education, stands opposed to both Jesus and the Old Testament:[10] "not merely the Old Testament belief and the living faith of post-Biblical Judaism are opposed to Paul, but also the Jesus of the Sermon on the Mount."[11] My claim here is that each of these claims is false and indefensible:

- There is no perennial Jewish debate with or about Paul through the centuries.
- The Jewish view of Paul before the modern period is anything but negative.
- Numerous Jewish thinkers have sought to reclaim Paul as a Jew—and in the process have managed to recover what I take to be the core of his original preaching.

First, through long stretches of Jewish history, there is almost nothing in the massive library of mainstream, Rabbinic Judaism. Efforts to find hints or allusions have come up dry.[12] Apart from a few brief references in Kara-ite texts, there is next to nothing.[13] In the early tenth century, the Karaite Jacob al-Qirqisani produced an account of Jewish sects and Christianity.[14] He goes out of his way to contrast Jesus, a righteous man put to death by the Rabbanites, with Paul, who first invested Jesus with divinity. He quotes Daud ibn Marwan, a Jewish philosopher of the tenth century who embraced Christianity before returning to Judaism and writing a treatise against the Christians. Daud names Peter and Paul as the true founders of Christianity; they laid down laws not found in the gospels and claimed that they came from Jesus.[15] As to Christian claims that Paul was a true prophet, Qirqisani responds that if Paul's teaching of the Trinity is contrary to reason, as it is, he cannot have been a true prophet: "it is evident that those who attribute the performance of miracles to Paul are liars."[16] That is all. Qirqisani holds a negative view of Paul, but he does not dwell on it.

THREE EARLY PIONEERS: PROFIAT DURAN, JACOB EMDEN, AND THE *TOLEDOT YESHU*

As for the claim that Jewish writers in later times, when they mention Paul at all, do so in sharply negative terms, this too is wrong. Let me cite three examples.

The first is Profiat Duran, a Jewish polymath who lived in southern France toward the end of the fourteenth century.[17] During a period of intense Christian persecution he converted to Christianity, but eventually returned to the Jewish community. Around the year 1397, after his return, Duran wrote an anti-Christian treatise, *The Shame (Kelimat) of the Gentiles.*[18] With a careful reading of the New Testament, he pointed out contradictions in the gospels and argued that many later Christian beliefs and practices could not be found anywhere in the New Testament—which is of course true. Students of Christian history today take all of this as a matter of course, but in the fourteenth century this was radically new in a Jewish author. Of course, Duran also wrote about Paul. And what he wrote is rather surprising. He goes out of his way to emphasize that Peter and Paul remained observant Jews. To support this claim, he quotes three passages from the Book of Acts (22:12; 24:14; 25:8) where Paul passionately denies rumors that he had told Jews to cease their observance of the Torah and that he had done so himself: "I have in no way committed an offense against the Jews, or against the Law, or against the emperor" (Acts 25:8). From these passages, Duran concludes that "he [Paul] had done nothing against Israel and was not disagreeing with the Torah or the customs of the forefathers."[19] And he asserts that "it would seem that Paul and his followers did not release the children of Israel from the Law and that there will not be found in all that they wrote that they believed that the Law would not be eternal for the nation."[20] Though he doesn't mention Matthew 5:17–20 here ("Do not think that I have come to abolish the Law"), he surely has this text in mind as his source. He then takes his argument one step further. After seeming to criticize Paul for emphasizing faith over deeds, he observes that when Paul speaks of the Law as no longer binding, he is speaking only about Gentiles. He sums up his position with these words: "he [Paul] admits the absolute obligation of the Torah for Jews, but for the uncircumcised [Gentile believers] only the commandments of the Torah [*mishpatei ha-torah*] are required."[21] As if to drive his point home, Duran sharply contrasts Jesus with Paul. While Jesus "did nothing that would disagree with the divine Torah" and regarded the Torah as eternal, he and his followers were nonetheless ignorant people (*amme ha-aretz*)[22] and his "madness exceeded that of all others."[23]

This is stunning. It will take Jewish and Christian scholars more than six hundred years to reach these same conclusions: that Paul never held that Jews should cease their observance of the Torah; that he upheld the Torah as the eternal word of God; that as the apostle to the Gentiles he preached that Gentile believers were no longer obligated to follow the path of Israel; and that the path of redemption for Gentiles led through Jesus, not through observance of the Torah.

So much then for the view that no Jew could see Paul in a positive light and so much also for the view that Paul had disappeared from the radar of medieval Judaism. It turns out that evidence against these claims had been lying in plain sight all along. We have been looking in all the wrong places.

A second case of a Jewish thinker who held a radically new view of Paul is the widely influential Polish Jew Jacob Emden (d. 1776).[24] Emden was a prolific writer who left a significant footprint on later Jewish thought. He was deeply embroiled in the controversies swirling around Sabbatai Zvi in the 1750s and is perhaps best known for his accusation that Jonathan Eybeschütz, a prominent Talmudist and Rabbi, was a secret Sabbatian.

Emden was like Profiat Duran in many ways: he had a solid knowledge of the New Testament and argued that Christians had misunderstood their own scriptures. Even more striking are his views of Paul. In one of his letters, Emden writes of Paul in a way that recalls Duran, though there is no evidence that he had ever read the latter's works: "the Nazarene [Jesus] and his apostles did not wish to destroy the Torah from Israel; God forbid." He then cites the famous passage from Matthew 5 about the eternity of God's Law. And he continues: "they observed the Sabbath and circumcision . . . for they were born as Jews and observed the Torah fully." Jesus and Paul came not to destroy the Torah for Jews but to establish a new religion for Gentiles. Gentiles were obligated to follow only the seven commandments of Noah, known as the Noachide commandments (Profiat had referred to these as the *mishpatei ha-torah*). In all of this, Paul was doing nothing other than following the Laws of the Torah as interpreted by the Jewish sages: full Torah for Jews, Noachide commandments for Gentiles—two separate paths to redemption, one for Jews, one for Gentiles.

The third of the early innovators takes us to a body of late antique and medieval texts known as the *Toledot Yeshu* (see chapter 5).[25] These are easily the most important unknown documents in all of Jewish literature. So widespread was this text in Jewish and Christian circles that it is not too much to speak of it as a Jewish best seller in the later Middle Ages.[26]

In essence the *Toledot Yeshu* is a parodic Jewish antigospel. The story line follows the narrative of the Christian gospels but everything is turned upside down. Jesus is the illegitimate son of Mary and a local skirt-chaser, though it is worth noting that Mary herself generally comes across in the *Toledot* as a sympathetic character. Jesus is expelled from his yeshiva for behaving insolently toward his teachers. The sages pursue and arrest him, put him on trial, find him guilty of blasphemy, and put him to death, not on a cross but on a stalk of cabbage. All of this takes place in part 1 of the *Toledot*.

In part 2 of the *Toledot*, which is not present in all manuscripts, the story continues with accounts of the apostles, just as in the New Testament Book of Acts. Part 2 finds the Jews suffering under Christian persecution, obviously reflecting conditions of the late medieval period. Desperate to end the persecution, the Jews turn to three great sages—Yochanan (probably based on John the Baptist), Shimon Kepha (Peter), and Abba Saul (Paul). After heavy negotiations, these sages are sent out as undercover double agents to undermine the new religion. They pretend to be Christians, but remain observant Jews. The centerpiece of their teaching is that Christians should imitate Jesus's humility and leave Jews alone—in other words, end the persecutions.

In most versions of the *Toledot*, Peter serves as the main double agent. So much so, in fact, that his birthday came to be celebrated by Jews as a major holiday.[27] When we ask how it came about that Peter assumed this role as a false disciple of Jesus, the answer is not that far away. It was not invented out of whole cloth. When we look closely at the gospel of Mark, we see that Peter there gets it wrong at every opportunity.[28] In chapter 8, Jesus calls Peter Satan. And in the last scene where we encounter him, Peter denies, with curses, that he is one of Jesus's followers.[29] It took little imagination to turn him into a pseudobeliever.

In some manuscripts of the *Toledot*, Paul appears alongside Peter as a savior of Israel. They appear in separate stories, one after the other, but they do pretty much the same things. They persuade the Christians to separate from the Jews and to leave them in peace. For this, says one manuscript, Abba Shaul/Paul earned a good name for himself in the world to come. Together with Yochanan, he built a shelter and a refuge for Israel. The text concludes, "From that day on the Christians separated themselves from the Jews and they were kind to Israel from that day forward."[30] And so, in the words of one Jewish scholar, Paul became a savior of Israel, a Messiah, who is not and never was a Christian.[31]

This is pretty amazing stuff. To be sure, there is a great deal of wishful thinking going on these texts. Paul never was a double agent of the rabbis; the Christians never did leave the Jews alone; and kindness is not the first word that comes to mind when we think of how most Christians treated Jews in the Middle Ages. But Peter is a different story. In this case, I think that the Jewish authors of the *Toledot* lifted the figure of Peter pretty much intact from the gospel of Mark. What was this thickheaded fellow, who denied that he was a disciple, doing among the followers of Jesus? To long-suffering Jews, the answer seemed clear enough. He had been sent to undermine the whole operation.

There is much more to say about the *Toledot Yeshu*. I think we have seen enough to realize not only that Paul was a regular presence in these widely disseminated Jewish texts but that he emerges there as a Jewish hero. Just as with Profiat Duran and Jacob Emden, and as in his own letters, he is both the apostle to Gentiles *and* a fully observant Jew. And the emphasis falls heavily on the "observant Jew" side. He poses as the Christian apostle to the Gentiles, but in reality he functions as a Jewish double agent whose sole mission is to rescue Israel from Christian persecution.

THE APOSTLE PAUL IN MODERN JEWISH READERS

In the time after Jacob Emden, there is something of a gap until we reach the nineteenth century, when things pick up with new energy. What do we find there? Does the stream of thinking that we have found in an earlier period continue in more recent times?

The answer is both yes and no. Two curious and closely related themes appear, beginning with Heinrich Graetz at the end of the nineteenth century. In his multivolume *History of the Jews*, Graetz initiated an entirely new strand of negative assessments of Paul—a strand that existed hardly at all in earlier centuries.[32] Graetz saw Paul as the enemy of Jewish people and an apostate from the Jewish Law: "Paul disparaged not only the ceremonial but even the moral laws of Judaism."[33]

Joseph Klausner, writing some fifty years later, adopts a similar position—Paul had abrogated the Jewish Law for Jews and Gentiles and rejected the Jewish people.[34] For Martin Buber, Paul is equally distant from Jesus and the Old Testament. David Flusser, in one of his early works, wrote, without any qualification, that Paul opposed the Law of the Jews.[35] And for Daniel Boyarin, a contemporary scholar of early Christianity and Judaism, Paul abrogated the Law not only for Gentiles but for Jews as well. He sowed the seeds that "deprive Jewish ethnic specificity (meaning here Jewish beliefs and practices) of any positive value."[36] I could cite more examples but the picture has become clear. Beginning in the late nineteenth century, a negative image of Paul entered the mainstream of Jewish thought for the first time and soon came to dominate Jewish thought for more than a century.

But at the same time and in every one of these same writers, there appears another current, flowing in the opposite direction. Thus Graetz could argue that Paul's primary concern was bringing salvation to Gentiles, *both before his transformation and after*, and that for Gentiles only the Law was no longer obligatory.[37] "Saul (Paul) may have recalled to mind a statement made by his teachers to the effect that . . . as soon as the Messiah comes, the validity of the Law ceases . . . Should the Messiah appear . . . all obstacles in the path of winning over the pagans are removed."[38] Graetz uses several different phrases to describe Paul's mission *before his "conversion"*: "to convert the entire world to Judaism";[39] the time was ripe "for the fulfillment of the prophetic promises that all the nations of the earth would acknowledge the God of Israel";[40] pagans would "share in the blessings of Abraham without the necessity of observing the Law."[41] Following his vision of the resurrected Christ/Messiah, he came to realize that the Law, which had previously been a barrier to the salvation of Gentiles, had been abolished. Pagans were "now in a position to share in the blessing of Abraham without the necessity of observing the Law."[42] But in the end, for Graetz, the apostle "over reached himself."[43] That is all. It is hard to miss the tension in Graetz's remarks. Did Paul abolish the Law for both Jews and Gentiles or for Gentiles only? On the surface, he holds to the former, but in his repeated insistence that Paul's sole mission was the redemption of the Gentiles, he comes close to the latter. The time was not yet ripe for Graetz.

In much the same vein, Klausner, who held that the only possible Jewish view of Paul was a negative one, goes on for pages about Paul's Jewishness: "He considered that he was bringing Gentiles into Judaism, not taking Jews out of Judaism at all."[44] "He was a typical Jew in his thinking and in his entire inner life."[45] And "it would be hard to find more typically Talmudic expositions of Scripture than those in the Epistles of Paul."[46] Even Buber, after opposing Paul to authentic Judaism, wonders whether Paul's negative comments about the Law apply *only to Gentiles*:[47] "this is the special concern of the apostle to the Gentiles—the Gentiles do not have to come through Judaism to Christ, but have their own immediate approach through him."[48] But he fails to pursue the obvious consequences of his own insight. Flusser, in his later writings, comes to a similar conclusion. Paul's argument against the Law applied only to Gentiles. His view was that "Gentile Christians should not live like Jews":[49] "one thing is clear: Paul uses Jewish legal arguments to establish his claim that Christians [Flusser means Gentile Christians] need not observe the law."[50] Gentiles, not Jews, have been freed from the Law. And writing on a passage in Paul's letter to the Galatians (2:15: "We who are Jews by birth and not Gentile sinners know that no person is justified by works of the Law"), he comments that any Jew would find it curious if a rabbi were to say, "You are redeemed by doing the Law."[51] And so for Flusser, Paul here stands in harmony with virtually all forms of ancient Judaism. To cite a more recent example, Daniel Boyarin insists that Paul remains an important Jewish cultural critic who demands attention from modern Jews. The dialogue in chapter 2 of Romans is not with Judaism as such but rather with an imagined Jewish debater who believes that mere possession of the Law was enough. Here Boyarin adds, in words that closely echo those of Flusser, that Paul "has essentially produced a sermon to which many if not most of pharisaic teachers . . . could have and would have assented."[52]

Clearly something odd is going on here in these bifurcated views of Paul. On the one hand, he is Jewish right down, as Klausner puts it (is he joking here?), to his physical appearance.[53] And yet, they cannot go all the way. I don't pretend to have an explanation for this split decision. Perhaps the tragic fate of Jewish communities in Europe made it impossible for Graetz, Klausner, and others to go all the way. Or, in the United States, perhaps it is anxiety over assimilation and the loss of Jewish identity that has stood in the way. Or it may stem from a lingering anxiety that by advocating an overly Jewish Paul one may be suspected of moving too close to Christianity. Here Flusser offers a clear example, though with a different figure. After lecturing on Jesus, whom he regarded as embodying the highest values of first-century Judaism, to his students in Jerusalem, he came to class one day and reported a recent nightmare. "I dreamed," he said, "that all of you who have been listening to my lectures went out to the Jordan River and got yourselves baptized!"[54] Yet another anecdote reveals the flip side of his anxiety. During a lecture on Jesus as a Rabbinic Jew, before a Christian audience in Geneva, members of the audience began to protest loudly. Flusser moved to take off his jacket, shirt, and tie to show that he was not carrying any anti-Christian weapons.[55] This is not a game where winning comes easily.

Whatever the reasons for this deep ambivalence, it does not tell the full story. There have been and still are other Jewish readers of Paul who are prepared to go all the way in reclaiming Paul as a Jew. Let me give just a couple of examples. Pinchas Lapide, who died in 1977, was a German-born Israeli diplomat with a lifelong preoccupation with Paul. In an essay where he argues for a new Jewish portrait of Paul, Lapide breaks completely with the old view and moves beyond any ambivalence.[56] How can we reconcile, he wonders, Paul's negative statements about the Law with a view of Paul as a Jew? The answer, he replies, is that *the Law is simply no longer biding on Gentiles*: "For Jews . . . the Mosaic law retains its full and unaltered validity."[57] Then, following his logic to its full conclusion, he makes the following comments: "He neither repudiated Judaism, as numerous theologians still maintain, nor was he the founder of Christianity, as Martin Buber assumed."[58] "Paul did not become a Christian, since there were no Christians in those times . . . he never underwent conversion."[59]

This is heady stuff. What separates Lapide from his predecessors is a willingness to follow one fundamental insight to its logical conclusion—that Paul is speaking to Gentiles, not Jews. But another factor at play here may well be that, as an Israeli, Lapide no longer lived under the dark shadow of Western anti-Judaism and anti-Semitism. But this is certainly not the only factor leading modern Jewish readers of Paul to new understandings. One striking example is a writer who is not a scholar at all. The renowned Yiddish novelist Sholem Asch is perhaps most famous, and infamous, for his trilogy on Jesus, Mary, and Paul. In his novel *The Apostle*, published in 1943, he presented a Paul who lived like an observant Pharisee until the very day of his death.[60] His transformation from Saul to Paul began while he was still the fiery Pharisee, as he overhears the words of a Phrygian Jew, "Yes, it is time, and more than time, that something be done for the gentiles."[61] Saul, as he was called at the start of the story, was focused on Gentiles from the beginning. What was to be their ultimate fate? Later on in the story, in a chapter titled "The Breaking Point," the narrator states that although "Paul preached to the gentiles that there was no need for them to obey the law of Moses, he was in his own life a strictly observant Jew." Though Asch speaks of Saul/Paul's transformation as a conversion, it all takes place within Judaism. The followers of Yeshua (Jesus) are called Messianist Jews, not Christians. Paul never rejected the Law and circumcision for Jews, only for Gentiles.[62] These views brought Paul into conflict with the Jerusalem believers and led eventually to an irreconcilable split within the movement. His new mission to Gentiles, about Yeshua the messiah and son of God, centers on god-fearers in synagogues. As for Jews, they must retain their traditional observances. But given Asch's strong commitment to religious universalism, he wavers on this point. When he writes his letter to the Romans, Paul is made to say that the Law brought knowledge of sin (Rom 3:20: "from works of the Law no one is justified, since through the Law comes knowledge of sin"): "the Messiah is the only one who can bring salvation from sin."[63] In other words, while Jews are obligated to remain observant, their salvation is through the Messiah Yeshu: "I say, those that are circumcised, let them remain circumcised. But if external circumcision of the body becomes the only gate through which there is entry into the Kingdom of heaven . . . *then the Messiah died in vain.*"[64]

These were bold claims, well in advance of his time, and Asch paid a heavy price in the passionate criticism directed at him from all sides. *The Forward*, the leading Yiddish-language newspaper, not only dropped him as a writer, but openly attacked him for promoting Christianity.[65] Part of the problem was timing. *The Apostle* appeared in 1943, hardly a propitious moment for an appeal to a Christian-oriented religious universalism or for a message that Jews should find their salvation in Yeshua. But at the same time, it must be recognized that on issue after issue, Asch anticipated positions that Jewish and Christian scholars would reach only decades later. And he did so pretty much on his own.

I conclude this chapter with a brief look at an American Jewish—and orthodox—thinker, Michael Wyschogrod. Although his doctoral training and most of his teaching were in the field of modern philosophy, Wyschogrod also received a thorough training in traditional Judaism, including tutelage under Joseph Soloveitchik. Early in his career, he became involved in Jewish-Christian dialogue. Not surprisingly, he soon came to Paul and sought to come to terms with his image as the chief source and spokesman of Christian anti-Judaism. His encounter launched him into a fifty-year engagement with the apostle. As he puts it in one of his early essays, "I would like to confess that it is difficult for me to see how a thinking orthodox Jew can avoid coping with the Paul-and-Luther criticism of the law."[66] For Jews living in a predominantly Christian world, he insisted, Paul demands a response. The anti-Jewish Paul of Western Christianity had posed a profound existential threat—and in the Europe of the mid-twentieth century a material threat—to Jewish self-understanding and Jewish existence. He could not be ignored. We have seen how this response took its different forms. Beginning in the nineteenth century, some simply dismissed him as a heretic whose views about Judaism could not be taken seriously. Others wavered, seeing him as fundamentally Jewish but corrupted by too much Greek culture. In more recent times, some have held that he was essentially right about the impossible burden of the Law and that he was the forerunner of modern liberal Judaism.[67] Still others argued that he had been misunderstood from the very beginning and that his thinking had been distorted in the course of later centuries. After all, Paul himself complains repeatedly that his congregations have misunderstood him. Wyschogrod himself appears to have belonged to several of these types in succession. But in the end, he found himself in the company of those who made a complete break with his Jewish predecessors. Here is how he describes his Pauline odyssey:

> Early in my career I could not understand how a religiously sensitive Jew such as Paul could speak about the law as he did . . . I could not understand why the fascination with Jesus led to such hostility to the Law of Moses, to the law of the Pentateuch. I was particularly annoyed by the idea that Jews think they are saved by deed while Christians know that they are saved by faith . . . it was simply not true that Jews thought they were saved by deeds or works.[68]

In other words, Wyschogrod could not make sense of the traditional image of the anti-Jewish Paul. It didn't add up. No "sensitive Jew," as he put it, could have held these views.[69] Over time, Wyschogrod reached a surprising resolution to his bewilderment. It certainly appears to have surprised him.

The Paul of Western Christianity, the anti-Jewish Paul, he concluded, does not fit the Paul of the letters at all. If you read them with care and in their proper historical setting, you get a very different Paul. The key to this resolution lay in Paul's mission to the Gentiles and in his self-designation as the apostle to the Gentiles: "The letters in which Paul criticizes the law were written to Gentiles who were being influenced to accept circumcision and Torah observance. In so doing, he emphasizes and exaggerates the dangers (for Gentiles) of living under the law."[70]

Finally Wyschogrod comes to the same conclusion as Lapide: "all of the nasty things Paul says about the law are intended to discourage gentiles from embracing the law and are thoroughly misunderstood if they are read as expressions of Paul's opinions about value of the law for Jews."[71] So also Lapide: "Of course, all of this (meaning something like Wyschogrod's 'nasty things') applies only to Gentiles. For Jews . . . the Mosaic law retains its full and unaltered validity."[72]

In the end, as he looked back over his earlier work, Wyschogrod seemed to hesitate, as if the old ambivalence had reasserted itself: "There was a time when I was convinced that this was the solution to the problem of Paul. I still think so but perhaps with less conviction than in the past."[73] His doubt here is hardly surprising. Twenty centuries of Christian anti-Judaism, with Paul at its center, weighed heavily on his shoulders. It was not a burden to be cast off lightly. But in the end he seems to hold firm, though he puts it as a question: "could it be that Paul was, after all, an Orthodox Jew?"

CONCLUSIONS, OR WHAT JEWISH READERS HAVE TAUGHT US

Whether efforts like those of Wyschogrod, Lapide, Flusser, and others will be enough to dispel the thick cloud of Christian anti-Judaism and to recover an authentically Jewish Paul, only the future will tell.[74] The recent works of two Jewish scholars, Pamela Eisenbaum[75] and Mark Nanos,[76] have brought the "new" Paul to a broader audience. The tide has begun to move in the right direction. But the tide has been moving for a long time. Tides move in two directions—six hours in, six hours out, with only a slight advance between cycles. It is hard to be optimistic.

In the previous chapter I raised a rhetorical question: could Jews accept the new view of Paul? Now it turns out not only that they could and can but that Jews were the first to arrive at this view, centuries before Christians and others.

3

LET'S MEET DOWNTOWN IN THE SYNAGOGUE

Four Case Studies

*They [the Jews] remained settlers, πάροικοι, a people apart,
with their own customs and religion which admitted little intermingling
with their Gentile neighbors.*

—W. H. C. FREND,
MARTYRDOM AND PERSECUTION IN THE EARLY CHURCH

THE JEWISH DIASPORA

BY the first century of the Common Era, Jews had lived outside of ancient Palestine for many centuries.[1] In Babylon (modern-day Syria), Jews first arrived as forced exiles, following the defeat of the Israelites by Nebuchadnezzar in 587 BCE. Less than a hundred years later, when the new Persian/Achaemenid empire under Cyrus defeated the Babylonians and allowed the Jews of Babylon to return to their homeland, many had become so thoroughly settled in their new home that they chose to stay put. A thousand years later, the descendants of these early exiles, speaking the local language of Aramaic, still flourished there and created a new culture of Babylonian Jews among the learned rabbis whose post-Biblical teachings became crystalized as the Babylonian Talmud and numerous other writings.

The same events of 587 may also have seen the rise of Jewish communities in what will come to be known as Asia Minor (modern Turkey). The prophet Joel (ca. 350 BCE) writes of Jews from Judah and Jerusalem being sold (as slaves) to the Greeks (3:4). Another prophet, Obadiah, (in the first half of sixth century BCE) speaks of "exiles from Jerusalem," probably following Nebuchadnezzar's victory in 587, who are in Sepharad. At a much later date Sepharad will designate the Iberian Peninsula, but here it may well refer to the city of Sardis in western Asia Minor, the site of an important synagogue (discussed below). There is archeological and inscriptional evidence for Jewish communities in at least seventy-five cities in Asia Minor by the fourth century CE. As for Rome and Italy, Jewish settlements there seem to have come rather late, perhaps in the late second century BCE. Jewish communities certainly existed in the first century BCE. Roman authors speak of them frequently. When Paul arrived in Rome as a prisoner he met with the local leaders of the Jews (Acts 28:17). Some twenty or so years before Paul's arrival, Philo of Alexandria led a delegation of Jews to plead their case against riotous mobs in Alexandria (40 CE). He reports that Jews enjoyed the protection of the emperor Augustus: "having been brought as captives (slaves), they were liberated by their owners . . . He [Augustus] knew that they have houses of prayer and meet together in them, particularly on the sacred Sabbaths, when they receive training in their ancestral philosophy."[2] By the fourth century CE inscriptions reveal eleven different synagogues in the city, while Jewish catacombs spread out under the city. In short, well before Christians appeared on the scene at the end of the first century, Jewish communities had established themselves throughout the Mediterranean world and beyond.

In Egypt, the Jewish Diaspora reaches back at least to the same events of 587 BCE. The prophet Jeremiah, along with other Jews, wound up in Egypt (Jer 41ff.), presumably under the protection of the Pharaoh, who had supported the Israelites in their unsuccessful struggle against Nebuchadnezzar. But we learn from a trove of Aramaic papyri that, even before the time of Jeremiah's self-imposed exile, perhaps as early as 650 BCE, a Jewish military garrison had been established in extreme southern Egypt, at a site called Elephantine or Yeb. Its function was to serve the Persians conquerors as guardians of Egypt's southern borders. These Aramaic papyri relate events from the late fifth century—internal affairs of the Jewish community and a series of hostile encounters between the Jews and local Egyptian priests, as a result of which the Jewish Temple, not a synagogue but a Temple replete with priests and sacrifices, was destroyed. What became of the garrison after these events is wholly unknown.

Following a gap of more than a century, the next phase of the Jewish presence in Egypt began under the rule of the Ptolemies, Alexander the Great's successors, who seized control of Egypt in 305 BCE and ruled there until 30 BCE. Early in this period, Jews came to Egypt in large numbers but under uncertain conditions. Were they invited mercenaries or exiled prisoners? It is not clear. In any case, Jewish communities sprang up in many locations and a particularly large community developed in the new capital of Alexandria. Jews soon adopted the Greek language of the Ptolemies and through subsequent centuries produced a large body of Greek Jewish literature. It was in Egypt that the Greek translation of the Hebrew Bible (Septuagint) was produced. In the period that interests us, the first century and beyond, when the Romans had displaced the Ptolemies as protectors of Jewish interests, Jewish communities flourished throughout Egypt. Sometime in the 160s, in the second century BCE, Onias IV built a full temple at Heliopolis, complete with priests and a sacrificial cult. The temple symbolized the important presence of Jews in Egypt; it lasted until 73 CE when the emperor Vespasian ordered it demolished. The jewel in the crown of Greek Jewish culture at this time was Philo of Alexandria, whose massive historical, exegetical, and philosophical writings, virtually all of which have survived, marked him as a leading light of the Greek culture of his age.

By Philo's time, the Jewish population of Alexandria and its environs had grown to many thousands. Quite naturally, Jews in Egypt had developed communal institutions—synagogues or, as they were called in Egypt, *proseuchai* (prayer-houses). As early as the middle of the third century BCE, an inscription refers to a *proseuchê* dedicated to the ruler Ptolemy III Euergetes and his wife Berenice. The surviving inscriptions and papyri make it clear these synagogues served a wide range of purposes, religious as well as financial and social. As for Philo, he speaks of them as educational centers, where Jews (and others?) gathered on the Sabbath to learn virtue from wise teachers.[3] There is little doubt that Philo's extensive commentaries reflect his own role as one of these teachers.

The number of synagogues in Alexandria is not known, although they must have been numerous. Philo speaks of "many *proseuchai* in the various sections of the city."[4] The most famous of those was undoubtedly the "great synagogue" described in the Tosefta and later Rabbinic texts. The version in the Tosefta, composed some two hundred years after the fact, reads as follows:

> R. Judah [b. Ilai] said: Whoever has not seen the double stoa of [the syna-gogue in] Alexandria has never in his life seen the glory of Israel. It is a kind of large basilica, a stoa/colonnade within a stoa, holding, at times, twice the number of those who left Egypt. And seventy-one thrones of gold were there for the seventy-one elders, each of them worth twenty-five talents and a wooden platform [*bema*] was in the middle. And a *chazzan* of the synagogue stood on it with kerchiefs in his hand. When one took hold [of the Torah] to read, he would wave the kerchiefs and they would an-swer, "Amen." And they would not sit randomly, but goldsmiths would sit by themselves, silversmiths by themselves, weavers by themselves, Tarsian weavers by themselves, and blacksmiths by themselves. And why to such an extent? So that if a visitor comes he can make contact with his trade and thus he will be able to make a living.[5]

Even granting a healthy dose of exaggeration, this must have been an im-pressive edifice. And like impressive synagogues in other cities, it must have attracted non-Jews. Here it is important to note that for Philo, Judaism was not just a religion for Jews; it was meant for all of humanity. The wisdom of Moses, as interpreted by Philo, far exceeded the wisdom of the Greeks; in fact, the Greek had stolen their philosophies from Moses. For Philo, the biblical patriarchs were missionaries and teachers to non-Jews, bringing them to the one true religion: "This is what our most holy prophet [Moses] through all his regulations desires to create—unanimity, neighborliness, fellowship, reciprocity of feeling, whereby houses and cities and nations and countries and *the whole human race* may advance to supreme happiness [*eudaimonia*]."[6]

I have little doubt that Philo saw himself as a latter-day Moses, bringing non-Jews to the higher wisdom of the Jews. It also seems likely that his instruction sessions included both Jews and non-Jews. At one point he appears to refer to such a student by name. The Roman governor Petronius, who refused to carry out the emperor Gaius's order to place a statue of him in the Jerusalem Temple, is described by Philo as "having had some rudiments of Jewish philosophy and religion acquired either in early lessons in the past through his zeal for culture or after his appointment as governor in the countries where the Jews are very numerous."[7] What is certain is that Philo held proselytes in the highest regard.[8] Speaking of what will happen in the final days of history, he gives pride of place to them: "The proselyte, exalted aloft by his happy lot, will be gazed at from all sides, marveled at, and held blessed . . . that he has won a prize best suited to his merits, a place in heaven firmly fixed, greater than words dare describe."[9] And he urges his fellow Jews to show great honor to proselytes: "While giving equal rank to all converts, with all the privileges which he gives to the native born, he [Moses] exhorts the old nobility to honor them not only with marks of respect but with special friendship and with more than ordinary goodwill . . . They have left their country, their kinfolk, and their friends for the sake of virtue and religion [*eusebeia*]."[10]

While there are no references in Philo or the Egyptian inscriptions to non-Jews participating in the life of synagogues, it seems more than likely that such was the case. Fifty years ago, Erwin Goodenough argued that several of Philo's writings were directed at Gentile readers.[11] Given Philo's strong admiration of proselytes and his view of Judaism as the ultimate religion of all humanity, it is hard not to see him as addressing, even teaching, a Gentile audience. That a Jewish school existed at Alexandria seems likely. That school must have included interested Gentiles. That Philo was its leading light seems certain. His writings must have served as "course packets" for his classes.[12]

In sum, by the first century CE, and increasingly through the following centuries, Jewish communities and their synagogues flourished in the Mediterranean world. Some of these communities were small, as were their synagogues; other were quite large. By and large, these communities were located in urban centers. Literary and archeological evidence finds them from North Africa to the Black Sea, from Syria to the Iberian Peninsula. Many of them had been in existence for centuries before Christians arrived. Gentiles were frequently attracted to synagogues; in turn, synagogues were open to and welcoming of Gentiles. Philo's boast that Gentiles shared in the religious life of Jews seems entirely justified: "Not only Jews but almost every other people . . . have so far grown in holiness as to value and honor our laws . . . for who has not shown respect for that sacred seventh day [Sabbath] by giving rest and relaxation from labor . . . and who does not every year show awe and reverence for the fast [meaning Yom Kippur] . . . and especially to that great yearly festival [= Rosh ha-Shanah]."[13] For Christian leaders of developing churches, these circumstances presented problems. The road to recognition and status was blocked. The solution was to attack the blockage. The result was anti-Judaism.

FOUR CASE STUDIES: THE BOOK OF ACTS, APHRODISIAS, SARDIS, AND DURA EUROPOS

THE BOOK OF ACTS

By now, it should be clear why I want to discuss the synagogue *and Gentiles*. It would be entirely reasonable to ask, "What has the synagogue got to do with non-Jews? Isn't it a meeting place for Jews?" By itself, the evidence from Roman writers should begin to change our views. It begins to look as if synagogues were in fact places where Jews and Gentiles did meet, regularly and for a wide variety of purposes. But so far, the passages we have looked at don't speak explicitly of synagogues. So where do we look to find evidence for Jews and Gentiles *in synagogues*?

We can begin with the New Testament Book of Acts. The second half of Acts (chapters 13–28) is an account of the apostle Paul's travel to cities in

Asia Minor, Greece, Cyprus, and Rome. The purpose of these journeys was missionary. As the apostle to the Gentiles, he traveled around the northeastern corner of the Mediterranean, preaching his gospel that Gentile believers had been saved by the faith of Jesus Christ. They were no longer outsiders to the goal of salvation, to claiming a share in the people of God at the End. What is peculiar about his preaching is that he regularly goes first to the local synagogue. And so the question arises, why would the apostle to the Gentiles, as he represents himself in his letters, go first to synagogues? The narrative in Acts provides the answer. Wherever he turns, he finds that synagogues consisted of a mixed congregation of Jews and Gentiles. And he knew this to be so:

- At Perga in Pamphylia (south central Asia Minor) he addresses Israelites and god-fearers (13:14).
- At Iconium (roughly one hundred miles northeast of Perga) Paul enters the synagogue and converts Jews and Greeks (14:1).
- At Philippi (northern Greece) Paul goes to the local Jewish place of prayer (16:13), where he baptizes Lydia, a god-fearer.
- At Thessalonica (northern Greece), he speaks in the synagogue (17:1) where he persuades "a great many of the devout Greeks" (= god-fearers) and "not a few of the leading women."[14]
- At Beroea (west of Thessalonica) he preaches in the synagogue (17:10), where he makes believers of "not a few Greek women and men of high standing" (17:12).
- At Corinth, he argued in the synagogue and sought to persuade Jews and Greeks (18:4).

The message is clear. Paul went to the synagogue because he knew that he would find Gentiles there. Both those called, in Paphos, "devout converts" (*sebomenoi prosēlutoi*) and others who, in Philippi, Thessalonica, and Corinth, are identified as "worshipers of God" (*sebomenoi theon*) and, in Antioch, as "those who fear or revere God" (*phoboumenoi ton theon*). Clearly these are all Gentiles, but why these labels? First of all, these Gentiles appear to be a regular feature of the synagogues. In just about every city that Paul visits, Gentiles are present in the synagogue in significant numbers. Beyond this, the labels appear to be titles, not just casual descriptions. In other words, these Gentiles were not just one-time, drop-in visitors but actual members of the synagogue community in one form or another. We will get a much clearer picture of these people, but for the moment we need to see them as Greeks who were both welcomed by and integrated into the local synagogue. And if we look more closely at the labels, it appears that there are at least two categories: one includes those who are called *prosêlutoi* who had become full converts to Judaism, full members of the Jewish community; others, called *sebomenoi* or *phoboumenoi theon*, were something less than full converts but were still connected to the synagogue in some officially recognized manner—later on they will be called god-fearers, or *theosebeis*.

One of the things we know about these god-fearers is that some of them were major donors to synagogues.[15] A Roman soldier, by the name of Cornelius, is described in Acts 10 as a regular contributor to the synagogue at Caeserea (Judea), the center of Roman government in the region. Cornelius is called pious (*eusebês*) and a god-fearer. From the same period, an inscription from Akmonia (in central Asia Minor) describes a well-known pagan woman, named Julia Severa, who had actually built the local synagogue there for the Jews. Clearly Julia was a god-fearer like those mentioned in Acts, but she was also a distinguished member of the local elite in Akmonia. She had made donations to the local version of the emperor cult. Julia's various donations add several important elements to our picture of Greeks in local synagogues:

- The texts from Acts and the inscription from Akmonia suggest that women in particular seem to have been attracted to Judaism.[16]
- Unlike proselytes, god-fearers, or at least some of them, seem to have maintained their old religious ties.
- The involvement of the god-fearers in the synagogue could take many forms—some must have been drawn by networks of Jewish friends and neighbors; some became financial donors; some were obviously attract-

ed by the strong sense of community that was missing in pagan cults; and some were there for outright religious reasons (more on this below).

Why, then, was Paul the apostle to the Gentiles preaching his gospel in Jewish synagogues? By now the answer should be obvious. Because he knew that he would find significant numbers of Gentiles there. Not only that, but these Greek Gentiles would already have become somewhat biblicized by virtue of their participation in Sabbath worship, in other holidays, and perhaps also in Philo-like classes. Since Paul's message was itself deeply immersed in biblical language and citations, the god-fearers would have been in a position, unlike ordinary Greeks, to follow his preaching.

There is every reason to believe that he met with some success in his efforts. But the other side of the coin—and this shows up quite forcefully in Acts—is that local Jewish leaders were not happy about this. In one city after the other, Paul is chased out of the synagogue and out of town, often with help from local civic officials.[17] His preaching caused deep divisions in the synagogue and in some cases led to near riots. After all, these leaders must have argued, Paul was an outsider and a newcomer and his preaching was creating a public disturbance.[18] What is more, in enticing god-fearers to leave the synagogue, the Jewish community stood to suffer a double loss: on the one hand, their prestige and social status would take a hit and, on the other hand, they stood to lose the financial support of the god-fearers. So it is not at all surprising that in one of his own letters (2 Cor 11:24) he reports that he had been in danger from his own people (meaning Jews) and that on five occasions he had received the forty lashes minus one, a punishment that dates back to biblical times (Deut 25:3) and was administered to Jews who had violated fundamental values of the Jewish community.[19] Some of these occasions must reflect the stories told in the Book of Acts.

One final question must be raised: How did these Gentiles find their way to the synagogues? Put differently, was there something like an active Jewish mission to Gentiles? Much ink has been spilled over this question, with strong opinions for and against the notion of a Jewish mission. But some things seem clear. First, Diaspora synagogues were open and welcoming. For them, the presence of Gentiles created a win-win situation. Good for Gentiles, who were brought close to the true religion (Philo), and good for the synagogue in the enhanced status and financial support that came with their Gentiles. Second, some of these synagogue buildings stood in prominent locations and offered dazzling interiors.[20] They were hard to miss. And third, there *was* something like a Jewish mission. Josephus tells of a Jewish merchant, Ananias by name, who visited the kingdom of Adiabene, presumably on business. While there, "he visited the king's wives and taught them to worship God after the manner of Jewish tradition."[21] Ananias was certainly not a full-time missionary, but he was spreading the good news. The gospel of Matthew (23:15) excoriates Pharisees (like Paul the Pharisee?) who cross sea and land to make a single convert (*prosêlutos*). Roman authors paint a similar picture: the poet Horace (from the late first century BCE) dislikes forceful poets in Rome and likens them to Jews: "we, like the Jews, will compel you to become one of our throng."[22] Dio Cassius (d. ca. 235 CE) reports the emperor's expulsion of Jews from Rome and states that the Jews "were converting many of the natives to their ways."[23] And Roman law codes repeatedly ban conversion and circumcision.[24] Finally, in the Christian *Acts of Pionius* (around 250 CE), the Jews of Smyrna are said to have invited Christians into their synagogue.[25] All in all, it seems reasonable to conclude that there were outreach efforts among Jews in the early centuries of the Common Era. Not professional and not full-time but outreach nonetheless.[26]

ANTIOCH

The most stunning literary testimony to Christians in local synagogues appears in a series of eight sermons preached at Antioch (present-day Turkey, Antakya) in the 380s by the towering figure of John Chrysostom, later to become archbishop in the capital city of Constantinople.[27] We are now in a Christian world, with a Christian emperor (Theodosius I) on the imperial throne. The Jewish community there came into existence no later than the late third century BCE. The main synagogue must have been an impressive site. Josephus reports that the Seleucid ruler Antiochus III had donated to the synagogue all of the brass decorations plundered from the Jerusalem Temple by his predecessor, Antiochus IV Epiphanes. The result, says Josephus, was that these "richly designed and costly offerings formed a splendid ornament to the holy place." And he adds that the Jews "were constantly attracting to their religious ceremonies multitudes of Greeks and these they had in some measure incorporated with themselves."[28] In the fourth century, roughly during the time of John, the synagogue was destroyed by Christians, the first of many such cases. One of the cities' synagogues was converted into a Christian shrine in honor of the Maccabean martyrs. Although ancient Antioch has yielded a rich find of archeological and artistic remains (especially mosaics), nothing survives of its great synagogue.

John is in an angry mood in these sermons. What set him off was the realization that members of his congregation were absent from church, absent because they were celebrating the fall festivals of the Jews in the local synagogues—Rosh ha-Shanah (New Year), Yom Kippur (the Day of Atonement), and Sukkoth (Festival of Booths). John pleads with the believers listening to him to drag their fellow Christians back into the church. He warns them not to tell others how many congregants were absent, for fear of public embarrassment. To drive home his rage, he paints a dismal picture of Jews and Judaism. He deploys the full panoply of the rhetorical skills that he had learned in school. High on the list was *psogos*, the art of insult and abuse. The synagogue, John roars, is no better than a brothel. It is the home of demons. Jews are wretched drunkards and dogs. No Jew worships God. To top it all off, he gives voice to what had already become something like a confession among Christian leaders: "If our way is true, as it is, theirs is fraudulent."[29] But like a good inquisitor, he interviewed the Judaizers to discover what drew them into their deviant behavior. What he learned from these conversations teaches us a great deal about what motivated these Christians. First of all, they did not share any of John's hostile views of Jews. On the contrary, they inform John that they attend the synagogue because it is a holy place, a place of religious power.[30] No one would dare to violate a business deal sealed in the synagogue. And if you were sick, a night spent in the synagogue could reveal a special cure.

"What makes the synagogue holy?" asks John. "The sacred scriptures are there!" they reply. Of course, Christians had their own scriptures, the New Testament and what they called the Old Testament. But there were important differences. As numerous images from Jewish synagogues and burial sites make abundantly clear, the Jewish scriptures were written on scrolls and in the ancient and mysterious (to Greek speakers) language of Hebrew.[31] By contrast, Christian Bibles were written in the language of everyday Greek, and a not particularly elegant Greek at that. In the time of John Chrysostom many Christians felt embarrassed by this Greek and sought various solutions to account for it.[32] Worse still, their New Testaments were written not on scrolls but in books (*codices*), a format used in all sorts of ordinary, secular settings. Tax records, business contracts, secular histories. No mystery here. The Greek New Testament was readily, perhaps too readily, available.

But it was not just, or even primarily, the sacred scriptures that drew Gentiles, pagan and Christian, to the synagogue. It was the Sabbath and the autumn festivals of the Jewish calendar—Rosh ha-Shanah, Yom Kippur, and Sukkoth—that drew John's Christians.[33] It is no accident that John delivered his sermons in the months of September and October. As for the celebrations of these holidays, we should not imagine that they were always somber days of rest and meditation. Various Christian authors, among them John Chrysostom himself and Augustine, complained that Jews desecrated the Sabbath by dancing and drinking.[34] In Antioch and elsewhere the Sabbath seems to have been a festive day.[35] The rabbis of the Mishnah forbade dancing, clapping, and slapping (thighs) on the Sabbath and during other festivals,[36] but the very prohibition points to these as common activities. In their later commentary on this prohibition, the rabbis of the Babylonian Talmud seem resigned: "We have learned: People should not clap, or slap, or dance and yet we see people do this and we say nothing to them."[37] John complains in his first sermon that Jews are subject to gluttony and drunkenness. On the day of fasting—probably

Yom Kippur—they are embroiled in a drunken party. They were dancing "in the marketplace with naked feet."[38] There is no reason to accept John's wildly exaggerated language about drunkenness, but neither is there cause for doubting that the Jews of Antioch, and other locations, celebrated the Sabbath and other holidays with dancing and drink. Shaye Cohen states the case clearly: "if Jews danced and clapped on festivals in fourth century Babylonia . . . we may well believe that Jews danced and clapped on the Sabbath in fourth century Syria."[39] All in all, the evidence suggests that we should not imagine the ancient synagogue as a somber place. Its festive celebrations must have appealed to pagan and Christian visitors. As we will see in the next chapter, Jews and Gentiles in Alexandria celebrated the Greek translation of the Hebrew Bible with a picnic on the beach.

Whatever the immediate effect of John's sermons, we know that they enjoyed a long afterlife in Christian churches. Robert Wilken has observed that "the sermons have been a factor in forming Christian attitudes in times and places far removed from ancient Antioch . . . The eight homilies were translated into Russian in the eleventh century at a time when Jewish homes were being plundered and the first pogrom in Russian history was taking place in the grand duchy of Kiev under Prince Vladimir."[40]

The contrast between John and his Judaizers could not have been greater. Their Christian identity was flexible; it made room for Jewish neighbors, their practices, and their institutions. John's sense of Christian identity, by contrast, was exclusive, with rigid boundaries. There was no room for Judaism, or paganism. John's efforts to create this tightly bounded Christian identity—which was always a work in progress—were profoundly threatened by his Christian Judaizers. Hence his brutal language. Judaism has become, in these sermons, the absolute Other. It was that against which John and others defined themselves. It was all or nothing, just as Ignatius had stated in the early second century: "It is monstrous to talk Jesus Christ and to live like a Jew."[41] But in Ignatius's time, and probably in John's too, these figures and their views probably stood in the minority.[42] Chrysostom also loved Paul. In his eight sermons against the Judaizers, he cites or alludes to Pauline texts some 180 times and mentions the apostle by name over thirty-five times.[43] In the Greek East and beyond, John's view of Paul as his ally in rejecting Judaism will dominate the scene for centuries to come.

APHRODISIAS

The city of Aphrodisias lies about sixty miles inland from the Aegean coast of ancient Asia Minor. The city survived into the seventh century when an earthquake and flooding led to its demise. The diggings there have yielded an impressive array of sculpture, inscriptions, and buildings. But no sign of the synagogue. We know that there was a Jewish community there, and thus a synagogue, from a variety of finds, among them a large stone column, standing a little over nine feet tall.[44] Where it stood originally is not known because it was reused at a later date in another building. One face, commonly referred to as face b, is covered with a long list of names; to its left, on face a, is another inscription.[45] (See figures 3.1 and 3.2.)

In fact, face b consists of two separate lists of personal names, many of them with professions or nicknames added (rag-dealer, grocer, confectioner, shepherd, bronze-smith, and so on). On the top there appear fifty-five persons, on the bottom fifty-two. The first two lines of the top list are missing but must have read something like "the Jews of Aphrodisias" or "the Jews of the synagogue" or, if this is a donation monument, "the donors of the Jews." The lower list has preserved its title and it reads, "And all those who are god-fearers [*theosebis*]," followed by the list of fifty-two personal names, again with nicknames and professions (athlete, missile-maker, fuller, sculptor, butcher, stonecutter, dyer, boxer, plasterer, and so on). One striking aspect of this second list is that the first six names are identified as members of the local city council (*bouleutai*), the political elite of Aphrodisias. Here again we find a Jewish community wide open to the local population, welcoming outsiders, and fully integrated into the life of the city. It is worth emphasizing again that the synagogue was a welcoming institution and attractive to non-Jews. The social traffic moved in both directions. Jews reached out to non-Jews and Gentiles came in significant numbers. This is not to say that all of the god-fearers (*theosebeis*) were motivated exclusively

FIGURE 3.1 Face a of the Aphrodisias column. Courtesy of Leigh Gibson.

FIGURE 3.2 Partial view of face b of the Aphrodisias column.
The first line below the blank space begins, ΚΑΙΟϹΟΙΘΕΟϹΕΒΙϹ
(AND ALL THOSE WHO ARE GODFEARERS). Courtesy of Leigh Gibson.

by religious feelings, but they were identified, and labeled, on a public monument as members of the Jewish community.

Face a reveals another inscription, shorter and somewhat later than the one on face b. This inscription describes a group within the synagogue called the *dekania*, or "group of 10," although more than ten names are mentioned. The purpose of the *dekania* seems to have been to oversee a soup kitchen for the local poor and to show their piety through praise of God. The text is worth quoting in full:

> God our Help. Givers to the soup kitchen [*patella*]. Below are listed the [members] of the dekania of the students/disciples of the law, also known as those who fervently praise God, [who] erected, for the relief of suffering in the community, at their own expense, [this] memorial. Iael the leader with her/his son Iôsoua/Joshua, leader; Theodotos Palatinos with his son Hiliarianos; Samouel/Samuel leader of the [dekania?] *prosé[lutos]*; Iôsês, the son of Iesseos; Beniamin psalm[-singer?]; Ioudas/Judas, the good natured one [*eukolos*]; Iôsês, *prosêlu[tos]*; Sabbatios the son of Amachios; Emmonios, god-fearer; Antôninos, god-fearer; Samouêl the son of Politianos; Eisôf/Joseph the son of Eusebios *prosêlu[tos]*.[46]

What I find striking about this *dekania* is that two of its members are labeled as god-fearers, that is, not full converts. Since the *dekania* was obviously an important group within the synagogue, the fact that it included two god-fearers indicates that Greeks could sometimes be fully integrated into the religious and liturgical life of the synagogue, even when they fell short of full conversion. Of course, the other amazing feature of face b, with its long list of names, is the number of god-fearers. It's almost fifty-fifty. We don't know what the exact purpose of the stone was—a membership list of the synagogue or, more likely, a list of donors on some special occasion[47]—but whatever its use, the rough balance between Jews and god-fearers on the stone suggests just how numerous Greeks could be in the synagogue life of this major city. And there is no reason to believe that Aphrodisias would have been exceptional.

Before leaving Aphrodisias, we need to look for other evidence of Jews in the city. And there is plenty. A bench in the *bouleuterion* (city hall) sets aside places for older and younger Jews (*hebraioi*) and further identifies them as members of the Blues, an empire-wide set of organized political parties and athletic fans.[48] Jewish graffiti are scattered throughout the city in shops and private dwellings, along with menorahs and ethrogs.[49]

One writer has called the discovery of this large stone "sensational."[50] Perhaps. But if we had not been so quick to dismiss the words of Josephus, Philo, Roman authors on Judaism, and the Book of Acts, we might not have been taken by surprise. What we find at Aphrodisias, from the fourth and fifth centuries, is the full integration of the Jewish community into the civic life of the city, and conversely, the participation by local pagans, of various social levels, in the life of the synagogue. Some of this, in the early fourth century, may have been encouraged by the famous Edict of Toleration, issued by the emperor Galerius in 311, a decree that brought to a close the persecutions of Christians under Diocletian.[51] But these relations predated and persisted long after that brief peace ended and lasted well into the time when Christian legislation sought to marginalize Jews throughout the empire. But not at Aphrodisias.[52] And not elsewhere. Long after the construction of new synagogues was prohibited by a law of Theodosius II in 415 CE, new buildings were going up, especially in Roman Palestine.[53]

SARDIS

When we move to Sardis, a city some sixty miles north from Aphrodisias, we find pretty much the same picture. Once again we are well into the Christian empire. The Jewish community there was well established already in the first century and probably much earlier.[54] The Jewish historian Josephus records several decrees from Roman officials and the senate at Sardis that shed important light on the community there:[55] the decrees mention that the city had granted a place (*topos*) for the Jews where they could decide their own affairs; another decree describes the many privileges that had been granted to them over a long period of time and orders that the market officials of the city should see to it that Jews have "suitable food"—presumably meaning kosher victuals—for them.

At Sardis we find a second "sensational" testimony to the status of Judaism in the world of Late Antiquity. (See figure 3.3.)

In 1962, archeologists discovered the largest synagogue in the ancient world, reasonably well preserved, along with seventy or so Greek[56] and a few Hebrew inscriptions.[57] The building is enormous—it measures more than 260 feet in length.[58] The main sanctuary reaches over 195 feet and the forecourt, with its lovely water fountain and three doorways opening into the main sanctuary, leads directly onto the main street of the city. (See figure 3.4.) It measures sixty-five feet square and was meant to serve as public space. The entire floor and much of the walls were decorated with polychrome mosaics and inscriptions. The sanctuary itself was lined by a

FIGURE 3.3 Aerial view of the Sardis synagogue. Lower right are the semicircular benches for elders of the community. Left center is the eagle table flanked by two lions. Courtesy of @Archaeological Exploration of Sardis/Harvard University.

FIGURE 3.4 Forecourt to the synagogue with public fountain.
The door at rear leads to the main sanctuary. Courtesy of George Ellington.

colonnade on both sides. At the far end, in the nave or apse, stood three
rows of semicircular marble benches for the community's elders, just as in
the great synagogue of Alexandria. In front of the apse stood a large table,
flanked on either side by imposing lion statues and held up by supports
showing large eagles. (See figure 3.5.)

In other words, this synagogue was not just enormous but hugely impressive. And it was located on the main street, next to the downtown
bath-gymnasium complex, which local citizens frequented to celebrate
their civic identity.

The building did not begin its life as a synagogue but was part of older
civic structures in the city center. At some point, the building was transferred to the Jewish community and turned into the synagogue. The date
of this transformation remains controversial. Some place it in the late third
century,[59] while others move it to the early sixth.[60] In either case, the final
form of the synagogue at the time of its destruction by the Persian armies in

FIGURE 3.5 Close-up of the eagle table with two lions.
In the background, the remains of the civic gymnasium and baths.
Courtesy of Paul Duff.

616 CE confronts us with a massive, open, and appealing synagogue, where Jews and Gentiles gathered, as always, for a variety of reasons.

As for the seventy Greek inscriptions found in the synagogue, nine name god-fearers who are also identified as members of the city council, just as at Aphrodisias.[61] Most of these date to the later stages of the building, from the fourth to the sixth centuries. The great majority of the inscriptions, including the nine whose donors are named as *theosebeis*, are dedicatory in nature, recognizing donations to the building and doing so in a public setting; they honored those who had made vows or pledges of support to the synagogue:

His family mosaicked (no. 2);[62]

Vow (or pledge) of Samoê, Priest and Teacher of Wisdom (*sophodidaskalos*) (no. 4);

Aurelios Olympios, of the tribe of Leontii, with my wife and children, I fulfilled a vow (no. 10)

Citizen of Sardis, City Councillor, and his son Zenon executed the ornament of *skoutlôsis* (no. 13).[63]

In addition to the nine inscriptions that identify donors as *theosebeis*,[64] other notable figures, some of them surely non-Jews, are cited. One bears the epithet "the most honorable" (no. 45) and three held important positions in the Roman administration—a *komês*, or Count (no. 5); one a former *procurator*, or provincial governor (no. 70); and an assistant in the state archives (nos. 13–14b). Beyond these, it is virtually certain that numerous other donors were Gentile "friends of the synagogue."

Here again—just as in Acts and just as at Antioch and Aphrodisias—we find an open and welcoming synagogue, with numerous local pagans, some of high status, who willingly identified themselves with the Jewish community. And just as at Aphrodisias, some of them received the honorific label of god-fearers. They had taken one or more steps beyond other Gentiles and had assumed something like an official status within the community.

Outside the synagogue, small finds indicate that Jewish shopkeepers regularly worked side by side with their pagan, and sometimes Christian, colleagues. As for Christianity at Sardis, its modest church on the outskirts of the city is a measure of the relative status of the two religions, as late as the early seventh century. As one scholar has put it, "there can be no doubt that the late appearance and success of Christianity in the province of Caria and its capital Aphrodisias is due to the very strong position Judaism had built up there in co-operation with the gentiles."[65] In fact, a Christian author of the late second century, Melito of Sardis, wrote his *Paschal/Easter Homily*, in which he proclaimed that Christianity had surpassed and erased Judaism. His hostility to Judaism may well reflect the status-imbalance between Jews and Christians in the city. If this is so, we have yet another case in which competition with Judaism led a Christian leader to embrace anti-Judaism.[66]

The last stop on our tour of sensational ancient synagogues takes us to the city of Dura Europos, fifteen hundred miles east of Rome, on the banks of the Euphrates River. Dura served as a trading and military outpost on Rome's easternmost border, facing the menacing Persians to the East. While the city had been in existence since the early fourth century BCE, there are no indications of when Jews settled there. But in 1932,[67] archeologists, digging at the western walls, came upon a synagogue structure decorated with what one scholar has called an "astounding display of Jewish art."[68] Not just astounding but totally unexpected, for the universal assumption had long been that Jews did not produce figural representations of any kind, in obedience to the prohibition of Exodus 20:4: "You shall not make for yourself an idol/image [*pesel*], whether in the form of anything that is in heaven above, or that is on the earth beneath, or that is in the water under the earth." Later synagogues in Palestine (for example, Beth Alpha, Hammat Tiberias, and Sepphoris), from the fourth century and beyond, with their images of Abraham's binding of Isaac and scenes of the divine chariot, had showed that the earlier prohibition had given way to some extent, but nothing pointed to what occurs at Dura. The three surviving walls of the synagogue are covered, floor to ceiling, with dazzling, multicolored panels of frescoes, illustrating and interpreting a wide range of biblical passages. Each panel is separated from its neighbor by an elaborate framework. The western or back wall, divided at the bottom by a Torah niche bordered by two columns, reveals thirteen separate panels, most fully intact; the south wall has preserved three full and two very partial panels; and the north wall shows three full and two partial panels.[69] (See figure 3.6.) The Torah niche is capped by its own panel, with decorations on each side and in the recess. (See figure 3.7.) Four individual portraits, two on each side, flank the two panels above the niche. (See figure 3.8.)

The Torah niche stands just over six feet tall; the individual panels range in size from 3′9″×15′3″ (Crossing the Red Sea) to 4′2″×5′8″ (Elijah at Carmel); the central side panels of erect individuals average around 4′×2′2″.

FIGURE 3.6 The front or west wall of the synagogue, with portion of the north wall at center right. At center, the Torah niche with two columns and panels above and on both sides. Scenes, left bottom to right: Triumph of Esther and Mordechai (Esther 6–8); four erect male figures above, left, and right of Torah niche; ideal Temple with Aaron and sacrificial scenes; Moses leading Israelites through the sea; ideal image of the Temple (*left*); the ark and the temple of Dagon among the Philistines (*right*; 1 Samuel 5–6); Samuel anointing David as king (*left*; 1 Samuel 16:13); Pharaoh's daughter rescues the baby Moses from the river (right; Exodus 2). North wall: Jacob's ladder dream (Genesis 28); battle at Eben-Ezer (1 Samuel 4); Ezekiel's resurrection of the bones in the valley (Ezekiel 37). © Erich Lessing.

FIGURE 3.7 Torah niche at center of front wall, with images above. Left: menorah, the chief image of late antique Judaism, with citron/ethrog and lulav, images of the festival of Sukkoth and its associations with the Temple and eschatology; center, façade of the future Temple. Right: scene of the binding (*akedah*) of Isaac by Abraham (Genesis 22), sign of the divine promise to Abraham's descendants, Israel. Above to right of Temple, hand of God. Courtesy of Yale University Art Gallery, Dura Europos Collection.

FIGURE 3.8 Above and right of Torah shrine; Moses and the burning bush with shoes removed (Exodus 3). Courtesy of Yale University Art Gallery, Dura Europos Collection.

These are large paintings and easily visible from floor level. The room itself, which represents the final stage of the renovations, measures roughly 45 by 25 feet and could have accommodated as many as 120 persons. A ceiling tile with an Aramaic inscription gives a precise date for the final stages of the buildings renovation—244–245 CE. Just eleven years later, in 256 CE, the city was captured and destroyed by the Sassanian Persians.

The attack by the Persians may be described, from our point of view, as a happy disaster. The front or western wall of the sanctuary stood flush against the outer defensive wall of the city. As its residents prepared to resist the powerful Persians, they filled the rooms along the wall with rubble, to create a bulwark against the invaders. The rubble on the back wall rose to the ceiling and then sloped downward along the side walls. The result for the sanctuary was that everything covered by the rubble was preserved, almost perfectly, while everything above the line was obliterated by time and weather. And so the frescoes of the western wall remain (in the National Museum in Baghdad) almost fully intact; those on the south and north walls, following the sloping rubble, are 50 percent or less intact; those on the east wall are discernible only partially at the very bottom.

Because there are no literary remains from the synagogue, we are reliant on the frescoes themselves and the inscriptions to learn the story of the Jews at Dura.[70] Two ceiling tiles, with Aramaic inscriptions, begin the story:

> This house was built in the year 556 [244–245 CE], this corresponding to the second year of Philip Julius Caesar; in the eldership of Samuel son of Yeda'ya, the Archon [ruler/leader]. Now those who stood in charge of this work were Abram the Treasurer and Samuel son of Sapharah,[71] and . . . the proselyte. With a willing spirit they [began] in this fifty-sixth year . . . And they labored in . . . blessing from the elders and from all the children of . . . they labored and toiled . . . Peace to them and to their wives and children all.

A second tile reads in part:

> All of them with their money . . . and in the eager desire of their souls . . . Their reward, all whatever . . . that the world which is to come . . .

assured them . . . on every Sabbath . . . spreading out [their hands] in it [in prayer].

Clearly these final renovations were undertaken as a religious task, with a view to a reward in the world to come. And one of the supervisors was a proselyte. By now this causes no surprise. Proselytes and god-fearers were regular donors to synagogues. There are no other references to proselytes in the inscriptions, although we may assume from this one case that there were others associated with the community.

There are a number of other inscriptions, in the form of twelve phrases painted (*dipinti*) directly on the panels in Middle Persian and three graffiti in Parthian.[72] These inscriptions were produced by Persian visitors, with Zoroastrian names.[73] The motto that best summarizes the content of these inscriptions is—*veni, vidi, admiravi*. "I came, I saw, I admired." Nine of the inscriptions refer directly to the panel on which they are written. No. 43 appears on Haman's leg in the panel illustrating Esther's triumph over the evil Haman:

In the month Miθr, in the year fourteen, and on the day Šaθrēvar when Yazdānpēsē, the scribe, and the scribe of the house *radak* to this house came [and by them] this picture [was looked at] [and] by them praise was made.

Nos. 49 and 51, painted on or near Elijah's foot in the scene where the prophet resurrects the widow's child (1 Kgs 17:17–24), take special notice of that scene: "when Hormazd the scribe came and by him this [picture] was looked at: [he said,] 'Living the child that had been dead.'" A graffito (no. 55) on the same Elijah panel, in Parthian and "generally beautifully written,"[74] exclaims, "Praise to God, praise! For life, life eternally he gives." And in one of the inscriptions (no. 44) a leader (*zandak*) of the Jewish community accompanies the visitors, presumably to explain the frescoes. This must have been the case on other occasions as well.

What are we to make of these graphic annotations to the frescoed panels? First, visitors came and admired what they saw. They registered their delight.[75] Perhaps it is not too much to speculate that the fame of the synagogue was widespread in the region and that it had become something of a tourist site, or better yet, a pilgrimage site, complete with local guides. Among these tourists/pilgrims were surely other Jews, in transit between Babylonia and Palestine.[76] Other visitors must have included non-Jews, for the synagogue was an open institution, with visitors of various sorts coming for various reasons.

In a recent study, Karen Stern has examined fifteen graffiti scratched onto different surfaces in the sanctuary, many of them of the form "may so-and-so be remembered" and "May so-and-so be remembered for good."[77] She views these as "recorded prayers or a different form of devotional activity," which were intended not only to be seen by other visitors but to be recited out loud by them:[78] "An inscriber's act of writing, combined with vocal repetitions by human visitors, then, might doubly assure a named individual's remembrance, both by humans and by the intended deity."[79]

And what about the frescoes? Overall, they are astonishing in their vigor; in the four standing individual portraits, they reach the highest artistic standards of the time. Whether or not they reveal a consistent overall program has been a matter of heated debate.[80] This need not concern us here. What is clear is that certain central themes run throughout:

- God's eternal redeeming care for His people: the exodus from Egypt and the crossing of the Red Sea (see figure 3.9), Elijah and the widow's child, the resurrection of the dry bones in Ezekiel, Abraham's binding of Isaac, Esther and Mordechai's triumph over Haman, and the well of Be'er.
- The centrality of the Jerusalem Temple and hopes for its reconstruction, whether on earth or in the age to come; the recurrent menorahs belong to the same theme.[81] (See figure 3.10.)
- The role of Elijah as savior-figure. (See figure 3.11.)
- The integration of Israel's heroes into the cultural world of the ancient world; this theme is amply illustrated by the patently Greek garb (chiton and himation) worn by Moses, Samuel in the anointing of David, the four individual portraits above the niche, and others.
- The role of Ezekiel, the resurrection of the dry bones, and the hope for national restoration. (See figure 3.12.)

FIGURE 3.9   Moses leading the Israelites out of Egypt (Exodus 8–14). Courtesy of Yale University Art Gallery, Dura Europos Collection.

FIGURE 3.10   The Temple of Solomon above and the future Temple below, surrounded by the figure of Aaron, the first High Priests of the Israelites, and scenes of sacrifice in the Temple. Menorah at center. Courtesy of Yale University Art Gallery, Dura Europos Collection.

FIGURE 3.11 Elijah heals the widow's child (1 Kings 17). Courtesy of Yale University Art Gallery, Dura Europos Collection.

FIGURE 3.12 Ezekiel and national resurrection in the valley of dry bones (Ezekiel 37). Courtesy of Yale University Art Gallery, Dura Europos Collection.

Herbert Kessler has argued that these themes make sense against the background of Christian anti-Judaism: "Surely it is no coincidence that many of the biblical passages represented in the Dura synagogue are among those made central in Jewish/Christian polemics of the late second and third centuries."[82] That seems reasonable. But were they more than that? What other work did they do? Claude Lévi-Strauss once defined myths as machines for suppressing time—the time between the myth and its later observers.[83] Lévi-Strauss might just as well have said myth *and* image are machines for suppressing time *and* place. The frescoes were not meant to serve as mere decoration and the sanctuary was not a museum. The colored panels were performative; they invited interaction with observers. And the sanctuary was a ritual space. It is not too much to imagine that with their remarkable brilliance and vividness, the fresco panels—in combination with the richly detailed ceiling,[84] the recitation of Biblical passages, the homilies, and the singing of Psalms (and liturgical hymns?)—were intended to transport members of the community into the biblical times and places re-presented in the panels.

Nowhere are these themes more graphically displayed than in the divine hand that descends from heaven in five panels. The point here is that God's providence governs Israel's fate at every moment—then and now. God has not abandoned His people; the covenant with Abraham remains with the Jews; the Temple lives and will return;[85] and the Temple sacrifices will be reestablished. In this sense, an atmosphere of optimistic messianism pervades the entire synagogue.

CONCLUSIONS, OR WHAT
THE SYNAGOGUES TELL US

Jewish communities continued to flourish long after Christian anti-Jewish rhetoric had pronounced their demise. Impressive synagogues persisted, and were constructed, after that same deadline. These synagogues attracted large numbers of Gentiles—and Christians—as proselytes, god-fearers, and Judaizers as late as the sixth and seventh centuries CE, despite efforts by Christian legislators to put a stop to such interactions.

As for the language of Christian anti-Judaism, Leonard Rutgers has noted that behind the rhetorical and physical attacks on Jews and synagogues there stood a dramatic shift in the Christian use of the term "synagogê" itself. Well illustrated by John Chrysostom but spread across a wide spectrum of Christian authors, "synagogê" came to be identified with Jews and Judaism as such. It "ceased to be an actual place" and was "abstracted into the very essence of evil . . . Henceforth, for Christians 'the synagogue' became the kind of arch-enemy that pagan or heretical Christian groups could never be."[86] Here again we find a wide gap between anti-Jewish rhetoric and social reality on the ground. Paula Fredriksen has put it succinctly: "Church canons censored social and religious mingling; imperial law lashed out at religious minorities, not just against Jews. To what effect? Our evidence suggests the usual gaps between repressive rhetoric and social reality."[87]

It is also true that not all Jewish leaders took kindly to converts and god-fearers. Some rabbis disliked proselytes, but even in Palestine they were probably in the minority.[88] M. Goodman notes that between the second and the fifth centuries "there emerged among some rabbis . . . a belief that Jews have a duty to win proselytes."[89] In the Diaspora there is little evidence of Jewish antipathy toward god-fearers and converts. In the long run, the kinds of pressure illustrated by John Chrysostom's sermons and the decrees of church councils probably made Christian Judaizing seem less appealing. But the doors never closed. In ninth-century Lyons, local Christians told their bishop, Agobard, that they preferred the homilies in local synagogues to the sermons in his church. He was angry. The result was an outburst of anti-Judaism and a bitter complaint to the emperor, Louis the Pious, about his favorable treatment of the Jews.

4

TWO STORIES OF HOW EARLY CHRISTIANITY CAME TO BE

What, then? Are you Israel?
—TRYPHO (A DISMAYED JEW) TO JUSTIN (A GENTILE CHRISTIAN),
DIALOGUE WITH TRYPHO

THE STANDARD TALE

WE all know the standard story of Christian origins and beyond that the story of the dramatic separation of Christianity from Judaism, the so-called parting of the ways. This standard story has dominated our understanding of Christian history from the early second century right down to our own time. Not just in Christian theology and piety but in scholarly histories as well. In its broad outlines, the standard view looks like this:

- Jesus of Nazareth was the first founder of Christianity. He broke decisively with the foundations of Judaism (Mark 7:19—"And thus he declared all foods clean"—is one of classic proof texts for this view, and I will come back to this text). The break was so decisive that it amounted to nothing less than a complete annulment of Judaism itself. In short, to be a Jew was no longer to be a member of the faithful people of God; everything about Judaism, including the old Israel and all of its institutions (the Temple, the covenants, the festivals, the Sabbath), was declared invalid. Israel was no longer the chosen people of God but now stood as a disobedient and rejected nation.

- If Jesus was the first founder of Christianity, Paul was the second. Paul's particular contributions were threefold, systematizing three views. First, the view that the religion of Israel had been declared null and void—the Law of Moses had brought sin, not redemption. Second, the view that since all of humanity—not just Gentiles but Jews as well—was lost in sin, the only solution was to be found in the redemption from sin brought about by the death and resurrection of Jesus Christ; there was no salvation except through him. And third, the view that God has rejected the old people of God, the Jews, and replaced them with a new people, Gentiles (*gentes* in Latin, *ethnē* in Greek), now called Christians. This is what makes Paul the second founder and in many ways the real founder of Christianity. I could cite many modern authors who have held this view but let me cite just two. In 1900, the enormously influential German historian Adolf Harnack put in this way: "It was Paul who delivered the Christian religion from Judaism . . . It was he who confidently regarded the Gospel as a new force abolishing the religion of the law."[1] More recently, the distinguished American scholar, E. P. Sanders has written this: "Paul explicitly denies that the Jewish covenant can be effective of salvation, thus consciously denying the basis of Judaism."[2]

- From the beginning Jews resisted and despised their own savior, the promised Messiah; they put him to death; as punishment for this crime, God brought about the destruction of the Jerusalem Temple by the Romans in 70 CE, thereby endorsing the divine rejection of the old Israel and the proclamation of Christianity as the new Israel.

- From this point on, or perhaps slightly later, relations between Jews and Christians come to an end; neither side shows any interest in the other, other than polemics. Jewish Christians have become heretics and soon fade away altogether.

- The earliest version of the standard story is contained in the very first history of early Christianity, the Book of Acts in the New Testament (probably written in the early decades of the second century); by installing Acts at the center of their Bible, Christians baptized it as the "official" history of the early church. The story in Acts begins in Jerusalem, the old sacred city; the main characters in the first part of the story are Peter and John, usually named together; interestingly, James, the brother of Jesus and a figure known from other sources to have been the real leader of the Jerusalem believers, is hardly mentioned at all. The main events that take place in the city are the lynching of Stephen by a Jewish mob; a severe persecution of believers, the result of which is that many disciples are forced to flee (chapter 8); the violent harassment of believers by a certain Saul, a figure whom we will meet again (8:3; 9:1); the arrest of Peter; and the murder of James and John by Herod Agrippa. The message here is unmistakable—Jerusalem, the holy city of the Jews, is a place of violent resistance to the true faith. It is a lost city. And it symbolizes the people of the city, the Jews, as a lost people. Here it is useful to remember when Acts was written: in the early decades of the second century, the Temple in Jerusalem lay in ruins following the Roman army's crushing defeat of the Jewish revolt, and thousands of Jews had been killed when the Roman army finally overran the city. Two miraculous conversions follow—Saul becomes Paul (chapter 9) and emerges a Christian believer, and Peter undergoes his own convenient conversion (chapter 10), as a result of which he abandons the laws of kashrut and in effect becomes a Christian. At this point, the scene shifts to a new city, Antioch, and to a new pair of characters, Peter and Paul. But Antioch also turns out to be the wrong place. It is the site of a bitter dispute between Peter and Paul over the status of Gentile believers in the community. Peter and his followers were insisting that Gentile believers had to become Jews, which for men meant undergoing circumcision and following other observances as well (Gal 2:12). Paul held a different view. He admitted Gentiles without any conditions, that is, without requiring Gentiles to become Jews. Peter and Paul had it out in

Antioch: "When Cephas [= Peter] came to Antioch I opposed him face to face . . . and the other Jews [= Jesus believers] joined him in this hypocrisy . . . I said to Cephas before all of them, 'If you, though a Jew, live like a Gentile, and not like a Jew, how can you compel the Gentiles to live like Jews?'" (Gal 2:11–14). So it quickly becomes clear that Antioch cannot function in the sacred geography of Acts as the new holy city. And so at this point Peter basically disappears from the story, along with all traces of believers who insisted on observance of the Mosaic Law. Paul takes over as the chief protagonist and makes his way to the new and final sacred city, Rome, where the story abruptly ends. Just when the reader anticipates a full account of Paul's activities and fate in Rome, the author breaks off his account; the real point all along was to get Paul to Rome. On his troubled way to Rome, Paul encounters repeated resistance from Jewish communities in the cities of Asia Minor (modern Turkey). His final words make the author's message patently clear— God long ago predicted and has now enacted the rejection of the Jews and their replacement by a new people of God: "The Holy Spirit was right in saying to your [the Jews'] ancestors through the prophet Isaiah: 'You will indeed listen but never understand, and you will indeed look but never perceive . . .' Let it be known to you that this salvation of God has been sent to the Gentiles; *they will listen.*"

This is Luke's version of sacred history and the birth of Christianity. It crystalized Christian anti-Judaism and turned Paul into its primary spokesman.[3] Some things Luke got right—Rome did become the center of Western Christianity, with Paul as one of its central heroes. But one thing, among many others, he got wrong—Peter did not disappear from later versions of Christian history. Not only does he eclipse Paul as the central figure in that narrative, but in later Christian legends he becomes the first pope and a Christian martyr in Rome. From the second century on, their names almost always appear together as if they had always been the best of friends. Clearly something is wrong with this picture. And the Peter who survives in the story of Western Christianity is a far cry from the

Peter of the gospel of Mark[4]—and Paul's letter to the Galatians. His image undergoes a total transformation.

The outline I have just given is sketchy but nonetheless comes pretty close to the standard popular version of early Christian history from the time of the Book of Acts to the present day. But it is not the only story, nor is it the earliest one. It will be my contention that the version told in the Book of Acts is both later than and a reaction to an earlier and a radically different story of Christian origins. Acts is best understood as a counternarrative to this earlier story. Without this earlier story, Acts makes no sense.

THE SECOND TALE

In turning to the second story, I want to emphasize three themes that run parallel to the first story: first, the rejection of Israel and the Jews as the chosen people of God, and their replacement by a new people and the emergence of a new sacred city, Rome, in the place of Jerusalem; second, the rapid and total separation of the church from the synagogue, of Christians from Jews; and third, the early disappearance of those believers whom many have labeled Jewish Christians. Out of convenience I will retain this label, but I should make it clear that I follow the lead of G. P. Luttikhuizen and Annette Yoshiko Reed, among others, in their insistence that it makes just as much sense to see these groups and individuals as subsets of Jews as it does to see them as Christians.[5] Jewish Christians worshiped Jesus as the expected Messiah (*christos* in Greek; *mashiach* in Hebrew)[6] of Israel and followed at least some of the Mosaic laws.

COUNTERNARRATIVES IN THE NEW TESTAMENT

Surprisingly, our second story has deep roots in the New Testament—not just in the numerous New Testament texts that run directly counter to our first story but also in recent scholarship on a wide range of New Testament texts. What, for instance, are we to make of the line in the Book of Acts (15:1) which reports that "certain believers came to Paul from Judea and were teaching the brethren, 'Unless you are circumcised according to the custom of Moses, you cannot be saved.'" Who were these people? Why did they insist that Gentile followers of Jesus needed to be circumcised, to become Jews, in order to be members of the Jesus-community? And did they disappear from the scene as quickly as the Book of Acts would like us to believe? We do learn something more about these brethren from Paul himself, who was deeply embroiled in a bitter controversy with them. His letter to the Galatians recounts his version of this heated affair. His opponents there include Peter, whom Paul accuses of hypocrisy, along with "certain men from James and a group that he calls 'the circumcision party.'" The issues at stake in the dispute are fairly straightforward: Paul's opponents insisted that Gentile followers had to be circumcised, to become Jews. Otherwise they were not "in." For them Jesus was the Messiah of Israel; redemption, for Jews and Gentiles, happened within Israel. One result of the split was that the circumcision party would not eat with Paul's Gentile believers because they did not follow the rules of kashrut. What is more, it is by no means certain that the so-called circumcision party was in the minority. In fact, it looks as though Paul eventually lost the battle in Antioch and had to leave town. Not only that, but as a number of his letters make clear, members of the circumcision party followed him from town to town, seeking to undermine his view that Gentiles were "in"—fully "in"—without observing any Jewish practices. And in at least one town in Galatia (Asia Minor), it appears that they had been successful in undoing Paul's teaching. In the opening lines of his letter to the Galatians he expresses his dismay: "I am astonished that you are so quickly deserting the one [meaning Paul himself] who called you in the grace of Christ and are turning to a different gospel" (1:6). So there were two gospels, one true (Paul's) and one false (Peter's and James's). The false gospel was the teaching of the circumcision party—Gentiles could be saved but only by first becoming Jews.

When we turn to other writings in the New Testament, we find surprising bits of information about this branch of the early Jesus-movement, the one that I am calling Jewish Christian. When we put these bits together we begin to discover another story, a branch that doesn't fit our first story at all. Take, for example, the gospel of Matthew. In a passage that will echo throughout many centuries, Jesus proclaims:

> Do not think that I have come to abolish the law or the prophets. I have not come to abolish but to fulfill. For truly I tell you that until heaven and earth pass away not one letter, not one stroke of a letter will pass from the law until all is accomplished. Therefore whoever eliminates one of the least of the commandments [the Torah of Moses] and teaches others to do the same will be called least in the kingdom of heaven . . . for I tell you that unless your righteousness exceeds that of the scribes and Pharisees you will never enter the kingdom of heaven. (5:17–20)

Here Matthew's Jesus emerges as what I would call a halakhic hard-liner, a pious Jew who insisted on total observance of the Mosaic Law (*halakhah*) and on internal states of purity. Any deviation from the Torah of Moses, even on the smallest detail, is enough to exclude you from the kingdom of heaven. And those who teach such deviations are also excluded from the kingdom of heaven. Here one needs to ask, who are those people who claim that Jesus came to abolish the Law and who teach that view to others? The leading candidate is Luke, the author of Acts. Many modern readers of this and other passages in Matthew have made the fundamental mistake of assuming that Jesus's attack on the Pharisees, not just here but throughout the gospel, amounts to an attack on Judaism itself. But nothing could be further from the truth. It is rather the opposite. Mathew's Jesus is telling his followers that the Pharisees talk the talk but don't walk the walk. His followers must do both. They need to outdo the Pharisees at their own game. Their righteousness must exceed that of the Pharisees. For the author of Matthew there is only one game—righteousness under the Torah. And later in the gospel, when Jesus attacks the scribes and Pharisees in a series of blistering woes (chapter 23), Matthew again emphasizes that the piety of Jesus's followers must exceed that of the Pharisees. The message is clear: the Pharisees talk the talk but don't walk the walk: "Stick to whatever they teach you, but don't follow what they do, for they do not practice what they teach" (23:2). This series of woes has often been taken as aimed at Judaism as such, but that is obviously not the case. The targets, as everywhere in Matthew, are the Pharisees and here also the scribes. What is more, similar criticisms of the Pharisees show up in Jewish texts of the time. Matthew's woes are thoroughly Jewish. The late Israeli scholar Moshe Weinfeld cites a number of rabbinic texts that reveal criticisms of the Pharisees (*perushim*) in language remarkably similar to Matthew 23.[7] One text complains that "there are those who preach well but do not practice well."[8] And as in Matthew (23:5–7), the rabbinic charges focus especially on the Pharisees' public displays of piety.[9] Weinfeld sums up these echoes as follows: "Accusations of Pharisaic hypocrisy in the gospels contain motifs identical with the accusation in Rabbinic sources . . . It appears that the critique of Pharisaic hypocrisy was a common phenomenon in Judaism of the first centuries of the Common Era."[10]

There is more to say about Matthew and especially about interpreters who interpret it as an anti-Jewish text. In recent decades, the tide has turned against this view. Along with others, the late Anthony Saldarini proposed a radical reinterpretation of Matthew's gospel, long known as the most Jewish of the gospels. Against this view, which recognizes Jewish elements in the gospel but insists that it parts company fully and decisively with Judaism, Saldarini argues that every element of the gospel, including all of its claims about Jesus, remained firmly rooted in Jewish soil: "He [Matthew] considers himself a Jew and fights for his interpretation of Jewish life."[11] It is not just a text influenced by Judaism—*it is a Jewish text*: "Matthew's group is still Jewish, just as the Essenes, revolutionaries, apocalyptic groups, and Baptist groups all remain Jewish, though sectarian and deviant."[12] Saldarini uses harsh language of traditional interpreters:

> To say that Matthew, because he accords Jesus such high status, is not Jewish, but Christian, anachronistically imposes on the later first century the clear identity that most Christians had created for themselves during the second century . . . to say that *Matthew's* emphasis on Jesus as the Son of God is incompatible with Judaism in the first century is to ignore the varieties of Judaism current in the first century.[13]

Put more bluntly, it is ignorance of ancient Judaism that enables interpreters to see Matthew's community as separated from other forms of ancient Judaism. More puzzling still, even those thoroughly familiar with the varieties of ancient Judaism seem unable to bring this knowledge to bear when reading the gospels. The barriers thrown up by this ignorance constitute a long story, told many times over. In 1921, George Foot Moore published a scathing review of Christian writers on ancient Judaism beginning in the second century and culminating in his own day.[14] His essay argued, and demonstrated, that "Christian interest in Jewish literature has always been apologetic or polemic rather than historical."[15] Sadly, it had little effect. Follow-up studies by E. P. Sanders[16] and Charlotte Klein[17] managed to gain some ground, if slowly. Saldarini builds on their efforts. His work is neither apologetic nor polemical. And it does teach an important lesson. Misreadings of Matthew have consequences. They have contributed powerfully to the foundations of Christian anti-Judaism.[18] And once established, they have proved stubbornly difficult to dislodge.

Or take the gospel of Mark. For centuries it has been argued that the statement of Jesus in 7:15 ("There is nothing outside a person which by going into him can defile him; rather, the things that come out of a person are what defile him. And thus he declared all foods clean.") creates a decisive break with Judaism.[19] These words have generally been taken to mean that Jesus thereby invalidated the Mosaic Law and all of its regulations regarding purity, even though it seems obvious that the final phrase ("And thus he declared . . . ") is a later editorial addition to the text. In short, Mark 7:15 amounts to the invalidation of Judaism itself. But is this so? The setting of this verse in Mark is a dispute with the Pharisees (the Pharisees again, not "the Jews") over washing hands before eating. That's the issue. Yair Furstenberg, an Israeli scholar, has shown that Jesus's view in Mark is that the hand-washing practices of the Pharisees were not biblical in origin but rather were a recent Pharisaic innovation.[20] Their practice is rejected by Jesus because it lacked biblical authority. In other words, this and other disputes between Jesus and the Pharisees are entirely intramural, internal Jewish matters. Moreover, in this case Jesus adopts a conservative stance. The Pharisees were innovators. Jesus holds true to biblical tradition.

To see his words as consistent with our first story is to misread them completely. Another Israeli scholar, Menachem Kister, has published a series of articles in which he demonstrates that a number of gospel sayings, normally taken as non- or even anti-Jewish, are in fact fully in accord with ancient Jewish practices and beliefs.[21] Of our saying in Mark 7:15, he asks whether the saying makes sense in the context of Jewish rules of ritual purity: "The plain answer is 'Yes!' . . . The similarity between the halakhic rule—that no kosher food can defile a man—and Jesus' saying . . . is striking."[22] Of the gospels in general, Kister adds the following: "Study of the Gospels makes it increasingly clear that their fundamental stratum must be read as a Jewish text, to be understood in the context of Second Temple Judaism . . . However, the original Jewish outlines of the traditions from which the Gospels were formed have become blurred in the Christian version of these traditions."[23] "Blurred" is a polite word here. "Erased" would bring us closer to the truth. And so it would appear that the gospel of Mark, read in its own time and setting, must be seen not as a text influenced by Judaism, but *a Jewish text*.[24] Daniel Boyarin has put it bluntly: "Mark is best read as a Jewish text, even in its most radical Christological moments."[25] If so, we have yet another document, within the New Testament, that runs against the grain of the traditional story.

Or finally, take Paul, the very center of the New Testament. I have already had much to say about Paul in a previous chapter (chapter 1). Let us briefly recall these passages from his letters:

Romans 3:1 ("What is the advantage of the Jew? Or what is the value of circumcision? Much in every way.")

Romans 3:31 ("Do we overthrow the Law/Torah through faith? By no means. On the contrary, we uphold the Law/Torah.")

Romans 7:7 ("What shall we say? That the Law/Torah is sin? By no means.")

Romans 7:12 ("The Law/Torah is holy, and the commandment is holy and just and good.")

Romans 9:4 ("To the Israelites belong the sonship, the glory, the covenants, the giving of the Law/Torah, the Temple, and the promises. To them belong the patriarchs and of their race, according to the flesh, is the Messiah.")

Romans 11:1 ("Has God rejected his people? By no means.")

Romans 11:26 ("All Israel will be saved.")

Romans 3:21 ("Is the Law/Torah against the promises of God. Certainly not!")

I will only repeat what I said previously: it is simply impossible to reconcile these passages with the view of Paul as the father of Christian anti-Judaism. They cannot be made to fit.

Before leaving this survey of traces of our second story *within* the New Testament, I want to add a few words about the Book of Revelations, known also as the Apocalypse of John. It is well known that this book barely made it into the New Testament.[26] Part of the problem was its intense apocalyptic eschatology; in the third and fourth centuries, when the New Testament canon was being finalized, the churches were no longer eager to see the end of history in the immediate future. Another difficulty was the book's rabid anti-Romanism. Christians, especially in the West, gradually came to see themselves as the true Romans, and by the end of the middle of the fourth century the emperor himself was a Christian. Anti-Romanism was no longer in vogue. But a third factor was surely the unmistakably Jewish character of the book itself. There is hardly a single passage that lacks an echo or citation of some biblical text, with the apocalyptic Ezekiel very much in the lead. As for the believers described in the book, their piety recalls portrayals of Messianic/Christian-Jews in other sources. John praises those who "keep the commandments of God" (12:17) and later issues "a call for the endurance of the saints, those who keep the commandments of God and hold fast to the faith of Jesus" (14:12). Here it becomes clear that John saw his community as belonging to the people of Israel. The "commandments of God" are those laid out in the Torah. His view of Jesus places great emphasis on purity, especially in matters of food and sexual relations.

David Frankfurter makes two important points about these passages. First, the mention of "meat offered to idols" recalls Paul's advice in 1 Corinthians. In response to a question about whether it was acceptable to eat meat first offered to/sacrificed before pagan deities/idols, Paul responds that eating such meat is fine, since idols are nothing, but that it becomes unacceptable if the practice offends other, weaker members of the community (10:1–13).[27] Second, fornication (*porneia*) here probably refers to intermarriage between believers and pagans, a practice specifically allowed by Paul (1 Cor 7:12–16).[28] The issue becomes somewhat clearer in 14:4–5, where John praises the 144,000 "who have been redeemed from the earth. It is these who have not defiled themselves with women, for they are virgins [*parthenoi*] . . . they are blameless." Here the sexual ethic of John's community moves beyond prohibiting intermarriage to honoring sexual celibacy. The closest analogies to this view appear in other Jewish settings from the same period: the practice of celibacy advocated in the Dead Sea Scrolls and the community of Jewish virgins, men and women, described and praised by Philo in *On the Contemplative Life*.[29] For John, loyalty to the commandments of God and purity of life defined the redeemed community. Finally, it has now become obvious that John's righteous anger is directed against Paul and his followers. Like other Jewish Christians, John sees Paul as the enemy par excellence.[30] In the end, the Book of Revelations, like the gospel of Matthew, is not just a text influenced by Judaism. *It is a Jewish text.*[31] Eccentric perhaps, but still thoroughly Jewish.

COUNTERNARRATIVES OUTSIDE THE NEW TESTAMENT: THE CHRISTIAN HERESIOLOGISTS

There is more to be said about writings within the New Testament, but I want to move on to the second chapter in this second story. Here I will look at texts *outside* the New Testament, texts which show that the Book of Acts got something else wrong. The so-called circumcision party mentioned by Paul did not disappear from the scene, as Luke would have us believe, for it shows up in various forms across the succeeding centuries. (Here I should add that I am convinced that he knew full well that they had not disappeared and that his account here is little more than wishful thinking; it is his counternarrative.)

The first text worth mentioning here is a passage in Justin Martyr's *Dialogue with Trypho*, dated around the year 150 CE, several decades after the gospels of Matthew and Luke. The dialogue is a largely fictional report of a debate between the Christian Justin and the Jew Trypho. The big question is: Who is right and who is wrong on the question of Jesus? Was he the long expected Messiah of Israel or not? Whose interpretation of Old Testament passages is correct? Do they point to Jesus, as Justin insists, or do they have some other, inner-Jewish meaning? At one point in the conversation, after Justin has argued that the entire Mosaic Law—and thus Judaism itself—has been annulled, Trypho inquires about a group of Christian believers that has come to his attention. Can such believers, he asks, who are circumcised and observe both the Sabbath and other Jewish customs be saved? Yes they can, replies Justin, even though they do not associate with other believers, but only if they do not attempt to convince other Christians (46–47). Clearly Justin has no affection for these believers but for him they are still "in." What is interesting for us is that such groups are still around in the middle of the second century, only slightly later than the time when the Book of Acts was written. Not only are they still around, they are apparently interested in persuading other believers, presumably nonobservant Gentile believers, to adopt their views. In other words, long after the disappearance of Peter and Paul, the old debates are still alive. The Jewish Christians have not gone away. But—and this is worth emphasizing—Justin is the last Christian writer who is prepared to say that Jewish Christians are "in." From his time on, Jewish Christians become heretics, complete outsiders. They are not saved. From that point on, we learn about them primarily in the writings of their Christian opponents, the heresiologists, who frequently and anxiously included them in their catalogues of Christian heresies.

But it may be worthwhile to have a look at some of these "heretics" anyway. Heretics sometimes teach us things that might otherwise disappear from the radar. The heretic-hunters seem to know many different groups, but here I will just talk about two—the Ebionites and the Nazoreans.[32] We first hear about the Ebionites in the late second century, when Irenaeus of Lyons (who died around 200 CE) describes them in *Against Heresies*. According to his account, their holy city was Jerusalem; they hated the apostle Paul because of the widespread view, by then well established, that he had repudiated the Mosaic Law. They told a denigrating story to explain his rejection of the Law: Paul was born a Greek; in Jerusalem he fell in love with the daughter of a priest; he became a proselyte and had himself circumcised, all to marry the girl; when it turned out that she could not marry him, "he became angry and wrote against circumcision, the Sabbath and the Law."[33]

Almost two hundred years later, another Christian heresiologist, Epiphanius of Salamis (Cyprus), writes about them in his treatise *Against All Heretics* (*Panarion*, 30.1–26). He seems to know several types of Ebionites and that they existed throughout Syria and beyond; he mentions Asia Minor, Rome, and Cyprus (his home territory). He reports that their leaders are called *archisynagogoi* (leaders of the synagogue) and that they referred to themselves as a synagogue, not a church. In general their way of life was Jewish. Their Bible was sharply truncated—of New Testament writings, they used only Matthew; they denied canonical status to all Hebrew figures after Moses and Joshua and rejected all of the biblical prophets. And, according to Epiphanius, they had their own versions of early Christian history: "they mention other Books of *Acts* in which there is much that is full of impiety."[34] Presumably these *Acts* told the hostile story of Paul the Gentile cited in the preceding paragraph.

The many reports (Irenaeus, Tertullian, Hippolytus, Origen, Eusebius of Caeserea, Epiphanius, Jerome, and Augustine, among others) about the Ebionites differ widely in their descriptions. However we explain the divergences, one thing seems clear. By the time of Epiphanius, there is reason to conclude that Ebionites had spread throughout the Mediterranean world and, like any religious movement, had spawned several different versions. They was no longer one group but many. And they were a continuing source of concern to Christians. As Andrew Jacobs puts it, the Ebionites "figure prominently in the project of defining orthodoxy throughout late antiquity."[35] Mainstream Christians used heretics in general, and Ebionites in particular, to think with and to harden the lines between themselves and dangerous outsiders. There was but one point of agreement between the heresiologists and the Ebionites themselves: they were not Christians; they were Christ-believers, but not like the Christians.

A second group or collection of groups that crops up in the heresiologists was known as Nazoreans.[36] Like the Ebionites, they followed Jewish practices and met in their own synagogues. They had their own gospel, perhaps a Hebrew version of Matthew, and regarded Jesus as the Jewish Messiah. Jerome, who writes in the early fifth century and seems to know a good deal about them, complains that "they want to be both Jews and Christians; but they are neither Jews nor Christians."[37] Like the Ebionites, they lived in Trans-Jordan. Indeed, the area now known as Syria seems to have been a lively center of Jewish-Christians groups. In that region and well into the fifth century, believers of this type may well have been the dominant form of "Christian" belief and practice. Philipp Vielhauer states that the gospel of the Nazoreans, cited extensively by Jerome, probably originated in "Aramaic-speaking Jewish Christian churches" that survived into the fourth century, quite possibly in the region of Beroea (Aleppo). And he adds that they were not "heretical" in that region.[38]

THE *PSEUDO-CLEMENTINES* AND A MUSLIM TREATISE

We cannot leave the topic of Jewish Christianity without a quick look at two sets of texts that lie completely outside the world of Christian heresiologists—the first known as the *Pseudo-Clementines* and the second a highly controversial series of passages preserved by the eleventh-century Muslim theologian Abd al-Jabbar.

First, the *Clementines*, which are essentially a long novel about Clement's search for true Christianity. The texts circulated in two versions (*Recognitions* and *Homilies*) and numerous languages (Greek, Latin, Syriac, Armenian, Arabic, and Slavonic) and were enormously popular reading in the

Christian world well into the fifth century and beyond. Embedded in the novel are several passages that point to powerful Jewish-Christian influences.[39] Let me mention just two of the most striking passages.

The introduction to the novel takes the form of an apocryphal letter from Peter to James in which Peter complains that his teachings have been distorted by Gentile Christians:

> For some from among the Gentiles have rejected my preaching about the Law/Torah, attaching themselves to a certain lawless and trifling preaching of the man who is my enemy. These things some have attempted while I am still alive, to transform my words by various interpretations, in order to lead to the dissolution of the Law; as though I myself were of such a mind, but did not freely proclaim it [the Law], which God forbid! For such a thing would be to act in opposition to the Law of God which was spoken by Moses, and was borne witness to by our Lord in respect of its eternal continuance; for thus he spoke: "Until the heavens and the earth pass away, not one letter, not one stroke of a letter will pass from the Law." (Mt 5:17–20)

This fascinating passage raises a number of enticing questions. First, do we know of any Gentile author who portrays Peter as abandoning the Law or Torah of Moses? We do. The New Testament Book of Acts, whose author was widely assumed to be a Gentile, does exactly this, as we have seen above. And who is the one described here as Peter's enemy? As Paul's letter to the Galatians makes abundantly clear, the enemy here must be Paul. In fact, throughout the *Clementines*, Paul, or, as he is sometimes called, Simon, is repeatedly presented as Peter's antagonist and an enemy of all true Christians. Are we surprised to find Peter citing Matthew 5 in support of his views? Not at all. By now we realize that just as opposition to Paul was a regular marker in virtually all forms of Jewish Christianity (the Nazoreans may have been an exception), the passage from Matthew 5 served as their favorite proof text, one that gave the authority to the view that the Law of Moses was both eternal and fully binding on all believers. In short, the *Pseudo-Clementines* represent a direct counternarrative to the New Testament Book of Acts. Writing of the passage in *Recognitions*

1.71.3 (Paul travels to Damascus with letters and promises to destroy the Jesus-believers), Annette Y. Reed has observed that although the passage echoes Acts 9:1–2 (Saul/Paul heads for Damascus, "breathing threats and murder against the disciples"; on the way he encounters the risen Jesus and becomes a fervent follower himself) "there is no hint of Paul's subsequent vision of the risen Christ or his commission as the 'apostle of the Gentiles' . . . thereby suggesting that Paul's apostleship and preaching are the *deceptive continuation* of his failed efforts to destroy them through violence."[40] Much as in the *Toledot Yeshu* where Paul also deceives the believers in order to undermine them. In both texts, Paul remains the zealous Jew.

Before we look at a second passage from the *Pseudo-Clementines*, let me make clear what should be obvious by now. Contrary to the Book of Acts and to the standard view of early Christianity, the believers whom we first met in Jerusalem among the first generation of Jesus-followers did not disappear from the scene once Paul made his appearance. They are very much alive and well in the fourth and fifth centuries—and beyond. More than that, they carried out an active mission to bring other Christians to their point of view and regularly challenged Gentile Christians on a number of fronts, most obviously on their rejection of the Mosaic Law. Matthew 5, embedded in the most popular Christian gospel, figured prominently in these debates.

Our second passage carries this story one step further:

> It is the distinctive gift of the Hebrews that they should believe Moses, but to the Gentiles that they should love Jesus . . . but the one who is from the Gentiles and has it from God to love Jesus should also have it of his own understanding to believe Moses. And the Hebrew who has it from God to believe Moses should have it also to believe Jesus, so that each of them might be perfect from both [meaning from Moses and Jesus]. (*Recognitions* 4.5; *Homilies* 8.5–7)

This is a complicated passage but its overall meaning seems fairly clear. Both Jews and Gentile Jesus-believers are "in." Both are saved. Jews by believing and following the wisdom of Moses, Gentiles by following the wisdom of

Jesus. In both cases, the wisdom is the same. In other words, these Jewish Christians, unlike their mainstream Christian opponents, did not deny that all Christians, even Gentiles who had abandoned the Law of Moses, are "in." But at the end of the passage there seems to be a third category, those who follow both Jesus and Moses. This I take to be a reference by the text to its own path, a path similar to the one carved out by the Ebionites and the Nazoreans. This path is the superior way. Jesus and Moses in combination trump Jesus or Moses taken separately. But, once again, unlike in the standard view, there is no rejection of Jews who do not follow Jesus. And in conscious opposition to the standard view, there is absolutely no rejection of Jewish observances. As the *Clementines* put it elsewhere, the only thing that separates these believers from other Jews is their belief in Jesus.[41] There is no clear line of demarcation between Jews and Christians and certainly no opposition, no parting of the ways. That will come later and, even then, fitfully. But here, in the fourth and fifth centuries, long after the Book of Acts, the relationship between Jews and Christians was still very much a work in progress. The lines of separation had not yet been drawn.

Now for the texts preserved by Abd al-Jabbar. In the 1960s Samuel Stern and Shlomo Pines stumbled on a polemical Muslim treatise aimed at Christianity. Along with anti-Christian barbs of various sorts, it includes a lengthy tirade against Christians who had been misled by Paul into rejecting the commandments of Moses and thus abandoning the true religion of Jesus. Pines soon became convinced that this tirade had been borrowed from a Jewish-Christian treatise written against mainstream Christianity.[42] The original document, according to Pines, was composed in Syria, in the fifth or sixth centuries. In Pines's opinion, the group that stands behind this treatise traced its history back to Jerusalem in the first century and may well have survived to see the rise of Islam. It central themes are as follows:

- The original gospel was written in the holy language of Hebrew; as the result of a quarrel between the true believers and the Christians of Rome, this gospel was burned and all traces of it lost; the Christians then produced a large number of gospels, all of which are false; they contain "many absurdities, false and stupid things and many lies and contradictions."

- Soon after the death of Jesus, Gentile believers began to abandon observance of the Mosaic commandments, despite efforts by true believers to persuade them otherwise.

- The leader of the Gentiles was Paul, a wicked Jew, who falsely claimed that he had received his gospel during a heavenly journey; in truth, he was driven by a passion for power among the Romans; his anti-Jewish teachings led directly to the destruction of Jerusalem by the Romans, under Titus, in 70 CE.

- Paul was responsible for introducing foreign, pagan practices, adopted from the Romans, into Christianity.

Pines's initial essay unleashed a furious reply from his now former collaborator Samuel Stern: no such document had ever existed; Jewish Christianity disappeared in the first century; and the entirety of al-Jabbar's text came straight from within the Muslim tradition of anti-Christian polemics.[43] This was a titanic struggle between two scholars of great stature. One element would seem to tilt the battle in Pines's favor. We know that Jewish Christianity did not disappear in the first century. The information provided by the heresiologists, along with the *Pseudo-Clementines*, makes it clear that such groups survived well into the fifth century and beyond.[44] But did they last longer than that? Patricia Crone has provided evidence that while some of al-Jabbar's material may have come to him from Muslim sources and, perhaps, as Pines himself recognized, from the Jewish *Toledot Yeshu* (see chapter 5), some of the material must have come from Jewish-Christian sources.[45] She speaks of Jewish Christians as mediators of Muslim influence in the iconoclastic controversies in the eighth and ninth centuries and beyond. She refers to them as "Judaizers" who had "gone over the edge to become Judeo-Christians."[46] And she locates these groups "in a Syriac-speaking environment, none earlier than the fifth century."[47] This is precisely the environment in which Pines's Jewish-Christian document could have appeared.

GENTILE AND CHRISTIAN JUDAIZING

In the preceding pages we discovered the varieties of Jewish Christians. They believed in Jesus, but at the same time they refused to break with their version of Judaism, which regularly involved circumcision, purity laws, and Sabbath observance. No need to make a choice between them. Better yet, it was wrong to make a choice. Different from this is the phenomenon of Christian Judaizing. Although Christian Judaizing is sometimes confused with Jewish Christianity, the two are really quite different. The one thing they share is the sense that Judaism was an attractive and living religious option. But Christian Judaizers remained Christians and pagan Judaizers remained pagans. Some may eventually have taken the next step to become full proselytes,[48] but not the Judaizers who, so to speak, dipped their toes into the Jewish pond—some more than others. They attended synagogue services, shared meals with their Jewish neighbors, observed the holidays, perhaps intermarried, and so on. But they did not convert and they were not circumcised.[49]

In fact, as we have already seen in chapter 1, pagan Judaizing predates the birth of Christianity. The evidence for the appeal of Judaism among pagans in the early centuries of the Common Era is overwhelming.[50] The Roman philosopher Seneca, certainly no lover of Jews, writes of the Jews: "The customs of this accursed race have gained such influence that they are now received throughout all the world."[51] In the Book of Acts, when Paul delivers his gospel message in town after town, he first enters the local synagogue and finds there a mixed audience of Jews and Gentiles. Some of these Gentiles became full converts—proselytes—but most appear to have been what we might call "friends of the synagogue," Gentiles Judaizers who found the local synagogue to be an open and attractive religious community.[52] And they were welcomed there. The Jewish historian and apologist Josephus, a rough contemporary of the gospel writers, writes, perhaps with a dose of exaggeration, that "the masses [*polus*] have long since shown a keen desire to adopt our religious observances; and there is not one city, Greek or barbarian, nor a single nation, to which our custom of abstaining from work on the seventh day, has not spread, and where the fasts and the lighting of lamps . . . are not observed."[53] And in his *Life of Moses*, Philo of Alexandria tells of a first-century holiday celebrated by Jews in memory of the Greek translation of the Hebrew Bible: "not only Jews but almost every other people, particularly those which take more account of virtue, have so far grown in holiness as to value and honor our laws."[54] And writing of the annual festival in Alexandria that celebrated the translation of the Hebrew into Greek, he reports that "not only Jews but multitudes of others cross the water to the island of Pharos to do honor to the place in which the light of that version/translation first shone out and also to thank God for the good gift [of the scriptures], so old yet ever young . . . some set up tents on the shore and others recline on the sandy beach and feast with their friends and relations."[55] Altogether this sounds a bit like an ancient beach party wrapped in a religious setting.

What is striking about the practice of Gentile Judaizing is that it continued well into the Christian world. Many Christians found the synagogue to be an open and welcoming community. But for many Christian leaders, of whom John Chrysostom is but one, Christian Judaizing posed a great danger, one that had to be eliminated. The stringent reaction of these Christian leaders to Christian Judaizing dates back to the early second century and remains a persistent voice for many centuries. In the first decade of the second century, Ignatius wrote a letter to the Christians at Magnesia, warning them not to Judaize (his term): "it is absurd to profess Jesus Christ and to Judaize."[56] Very quickly, Christian leaders moved to the view that Christianity and Judaism were polar opposites. Truth became an all-or-nothing matter. And the repeated decrees issued by bishops and church councils denouncing the practice of Judaizing are proof of just how widespread this view was.[57]

Thus far, I have focused on what we might call Western Christianity, both Greek and Latin, ranging from Rome in the West to Antioch in the East. In chapter 3, we examined the physical remains of a synagogue in the East (Dura Europos, on the Euphrates); but here it is worth making a detour to look briefly at two Eastern Christian writers, both of whom wrote in Syriac: Aphrahat (d. ca. 345) who lived and wrote in eastern Syria, under Persian rule, and Ephrem Syrus (d. ca. 373) who was active in western Syria, at Nisibis, under Roman rule. Aphrahat's twenty-three *Demonstrations* discuss a wide range of issues; in nineteen of them, he discusses relations between Christians and Jews, or rather between the church and Israel.[58] Like virtually all Christian writers, he is a thoroughgoing supercessionist. Christianity is the true faith; Israel has been rejected. But on numerous occasions, Aphrahat reveals that Judaism in his neighborhood is very much alive and active, both in raising objections to Christians claims and in persuading Christians to accede to Jewish criticisms.[59] Jacob Neusner describes the relationship between Jews and Christians in the region as "vigorous, intimate, and competitive." Here, under Persian rule, with no protection from a Roman government, Christians lived as an anxious, persecuted minority, while Jews made use of their relatively superior position to press their case, emphasizing Christian ties to Persia's Roman enemy to the West and arguing that Israel remained the chosen people. Aphrahat speaks of "the sage of the Jews" who disputes Christian interpretations of biblical texts, appeals to the common people with his disturbing arguments, and denies that God hears the prayers of Christians:[60] "It happened one day a man who is called 'the sage of the Jews' met me and asked, saying, . . . 'There is not among your (Christian) entire people one wise man whose prayer is listened to, who seeks from God that your persecutions should cease.'"[61]

Thus it is not surprising that a recurrent theme in the *Demonstrations* is that believers should be ready to counter Jewish arguments. If we judge by the amount of space given to Jewish criticisms, the matter was urgent. Some of the believers were wavering. Although the *Demonstrations* give no direct evidence of Christians defecting to or even visiting synagogues, it is not too much to imagine that some Christians, weakened in their faith by Jewish critics and suffering from Persian persecution, probably sought refuge by associating themselves with Jewish communities. As we have seen in the preceding pages, there is plenty of evidence for Jewish Christians in the region who would have stood much closer to Judaism than Aphrahat would have allowed. Nor should we forget that Christians in Mesopotamia, as elsewhere, may have been attracted to synagogues for other reasons as well.

Ephrem the Syrian presents us with an altogether different case. His tone is radically different from that of Aphrahat. In his classic essay "The

Jews in the Works of the Church Fathers," Samuel Krauss writes this of Ephrem:

> In passionate hatred of the Jews, in contempt and active hostility towards the people of the covenant, Ephrem of Syria surpasses all the Church Fathers who came before and all those who went after him. His voluminous writings are filled with rage and animosity against the Jews. He would like to destroy them with the fire of his words and to draw down upon their heads, by his prayers, the avenging lightning of an offended deity.[62]

Aphrahat represents a classic case of Christian anti-Judaism: Christianity has replaced Judaism; Jewish beliefs and practices are no longer valid. But his language is devoid of the violent, irrational speech that pervades the sermons of John Chrysostom,[63] and the liturgical poems of Ephrem. Here the mood, the tone, the language of Ephrem is totally different. This is no longer anti-Judaism, but anti-Semitism.[64] His Syriac hymns, meant to be recited during worship, both reflect and are meant to reinforce a hostile view of Jews and Judaism among the faithful. Studies of Ephrem's works by Christine Shepardson[65] and Kathleen McVey[66] have shown that hostile views of Jews and Judaism lurk in every corner of Ephrem's work. Shepardson describes Ephrem's nineteenth hymn, *On Unleavened Bread*, as follows:

> In this hymn Ephrem touts some of the most vitriolic anti-Jewish imagery in his repertoire, combining the insulting images of the Jews as an evil and rejected people that stinks like garlic and onions with explicit warnings about the deadly threat that the Jews pose to those who would partake of the Christian Eucharist in his church . . . Jews eat unleavened bread, which is a "deadly drug," while Christians eat the Eucharist, which is the "drug of life."[67]

What forces led Ephrem to these bilious heights? In some respects, we have already encountered them in John Chrysostom: the fact that members of his own congregation participated in the life of the synagogue stood in flagrant contradiction with his claim that the Jews were a dead people.

Christian triumphalism could not tolerate a vibrant Judaism, much less Christians in their midst who found Judaism appealing.[68] Next, the aborted efforts of the emperor Julian, in 363 CE, to rebuild the Temple in Jerusalem. Julian, the ex-Christian, knew full well the role played by the lost Temple in Christian anti-Judaism and set out to reverse the argument that the destruction of the Temple marked the decisive divine judgment against the Jews. Ephrem quotes the response of some Jews to Julian's efforts and the widespread hope, amply attested in the mosaics of late antique synagogues, that the Temple would be rebuilt and Jerusalem reestablished:

> Now, look! This people dreams that it will return; the people which angered God in all that it did awaits and demands a time when it will have satisfaction. As soon as this people hears of a return, they lift up their voices and shout, "Jerusalem will be rebuilt!" Again and again they listen, for they long for the return. "The fame of the capital will be great; its name will be glorious," they repeatedly exclaim.[69]

Although the rebuilding effort failed, the very attempt sent shivers through the Christian world across decades and centuries.[70] Krauss also noted the strong influence of Jewish biblical interpretations (*aggadot*) in a number of Ephrem's own commentaries.[71] Here we encounter a strong case of the anxiety of influence. However these Jewish influences may have come to him, their source—Judaism—was the very antithesis of the true faith. Anxiety thus turned into denial and hatred. Finally, McVey has shown that in his *Hymns on the Nativity*, Ephrem attacks "slanderers among the Jews" who had insisted that Jesus was born of human seed and that the resurrection was nothing but a stolen body (*Hymn* 10.9). These and other "slanders" strongly suggest that Ephrem was familiar with, and responding to, an early version of the *Toledot Yeshu*, which makes precisely these claims: "doubts about the virginal conception, Joseph's confusion, Jesus' lowly status as 'son of a carpenter,' and the suggestion that the empty tomb was a hoax."[72]

At times, Christian anti-Judaism and anti-Semitism passed from words to deeds. The destruction of a synagogue in 388 in Mesopotamia by a bishop and his followers[73] and the disappearance of the synagogue in Antioch are but two examples of widespread Christian expropriation and destruction of synagogues.[74] This, too, despite Christian laws prohibiting harm to synagogues.[75] We are now in a much better position to understand Christian assaults on synagogues. By their very existence, and even more by virtue of their appeal to pagans and Christians alike, they put the lie to Christian triumphalist rhetoric. They had to be eliminated, in word and deed.

But the reality on the ground was altogether different. In his important essay "Christian Emperors, Christian Church and the Jews of the Diaspora in the Greek East, CE 379–450," Fergus Millar has gathered an impressive body of evidence—archeological, epigraphic, and literary—to show that in the Greek East, roughly east of a line drawn from Antioch to Alexandria, Christians felt the presence of Jews as a serious counterforce, a force both imagined and real.[76] New synagogues were built; pagans and Christians continued to frequent synagogues; Jews confronted Christians on a number of theological issues; and on occasion, Jews undertook public acts of "ritualized expressions of hostility, or actual violence" against Christians.[77] Jewish communities were anything but isolated and powerless minorities: "We need to realize that a Jewish Diaspora in an emphatically Christian empire . . . seems to show it as numerous, active and confident (and even on occasion aggressive)" and that this Eastern Diaspora represents "a quite new and distinctive phase in religious history."[78]

Let me close this chapter with an example of Christian Judaizing closer to our own time. On January 5, 1988, the English-language newspaper *The Jerusalem Post* published a story about a French nun, Sister Marie Catherine, mother superior of a convent that she created. After an emotional pilgrimage to Israel in 1985, she learned from her mother that she had been born Jewish and that her family had converted to Christianity during World War II to protect Marie from persecution by the Nazis.[79] These powerful experiences caused Marie Catherine to change her name to Mother Myriam and to introduce dramatic changes in her convent. The sisters began to follow the laws of kashrut, placed a mezuzah at the entrance, and observed the Jewish Sabbath and other Jewish holidays, all of this alongside their normal Christian observances. And Mother Myriam renamed the order The Little Sisters of Israel. When the local religious authorities learned of these changes they were not happy. Her transgressive behavior, her willingness to mix categories, and her readiness to cross forbidden boundaries got her into a heap of trouble with the religious authorities—both Christian and Jewish. The Roman Catholic cardinal of Lyon decreed that Jews had to be good Jews and Christians good Christians. The cardinal was not alone in these sentiments. The chief rabbi of the region insisted that Mother Myriam had to choose between being a good Jew or a good Christian. Not only are the two statements virtually identical with each other but they recall the words of Jerome more than fifteen hundred years earlier, who said of the Nazoreans, "They want to be both Jews and Christians but are neither." Recall also the words of Epiphanius who reports that they refused to be called either Jews or Christians: "They are Jews and nothing else."[80] Here we can only exclaim, "The more some things change, the more they stay the same."

CONCLUSIONS, OR WHAT THE TWO TALES TELL US

The standard view of early Christian history—a view that has dominated popular views as well as much of traditional scholarship—tells at best a partial truth and at worst a seriously distorted one. Yet it has showed a remarkable persistence: "The fact that scholars *keep* having to tell this new story shows there is something perniciously compelling about the 'standard view.'"[81] Contrary to the view presented by Christian heresiologists, Jewish Christians were not a beleaguered and isolated minority in the early centuries. In certain regions, Syria in particular, they were not a tiny minority. There it was not a matter of a confident, dominant orthodox majority confronting a heretical minority. Jewish Christians *were* the orthodox.[82] In short, when we enter geography into the equation, the issue of orthodoxy and heresy becomes complicated.[83] The same applies to different times. Orthodoxy was not a massive, all-consuming force that swept away all competitors. Perhaps in the minds of its defenders, but not on the ground. Joan Taylor has observed that the fourth century, not the first or the second, witnessed a "widespread interest in Jewish praxis by

Gentile members of the church and a variety of groups exhibiting 'Jewish-Christian' characteristics."[84] It is surely no coincidence that, in the fourth century, heresiologists (for example, Jerome and Epiphanius) focused on refuting Jewish Christians (and others) and that, in the same period, the evidence for Judaizing Christians becomes abundant.

Our second story, in its several versions, has revealed an altogether different view of relations between Christians and Jews. While Christian elites (theologians and bishops) trumpeted their anti-Judaism, many other Christians saw things in a different light. And the two views are intimately connected. Down to at least the late fourth century, these "other" Christians viewed Judaism as an attractive religious option: some went all the way and became Jewish Christians; some went part way as Judaizers. None of this fits the standard story. As the recent volume *The Ways That Never Parted: Jews and Christians in Late Antiquity and the Early Middle Ages* has argued, relations between Jews and Christians did not follow a straight line from early engagement to later separation.[85] When the factors of times, geography, politics, and social status enter the picture, straight lines disappear. At this point, we find not just two stories but many.

As for the synagogues, they were open and welcoming Jewish communities, both before the arrival of Christianity and after.[86] This too flies in the face of the standard story, which holds that Judaism quickly withered away and survived the rise of Christianity in a state of miserable isolation. Jews were not interested in outsiders and outsiders were not attracted to Judaism. But the long-standing practice of pagan and Christian Judaizing shows just how wrong this picture was.

We are now in a better position to understand what it was about Judaizing and Jewish Christianity that so irritated Jerome and Epiphanius in earlier centuries and the cardinal and the rabbi in the twentieth. Religious elites have little tolerance for ambivalence or ambiguity. They seek to create tightly defined categories. They insist that you must be in or out. There are no in-betweens, no hybrids. Any attempt to cross these boundaries or to mix the categories sets off loud alarms. Such things threaten the whole business. They are dangerous and destabilizing; they must be eliminated. They become heresies, outsiders, not us. So it was with the fate of Jewish

Christianity. While Justin Martyr in the second century could affirm that Jewish Christians were still "in," the boundaries became increasingly firm in later centuries as bishops and theologians built a powerful political institution, the church. From then on, these elites attempted to prevent any form of boundary-crossing, especially with Jews. Jews and their Jewish-Christian cousins were the truly dangerous ones. They probed unresolved Christian anxieties regarding Jewish criticisms of Christianity on the one side and questions raised within the churches on the other: "If Jesus was circumcised, why aren't we?"[87] "If Jesus required observance of the Mosaic Law (as in Matthew 5), why don't we?" Those who dared to enter the doors of welcoming and flourishing synagogues did so increasingly at great risk. But as the case of Mother Myriam tells us, the efforts of these religious elites were never fully successful.

Roman legal documents point in the same direction. Numerous laws were enacted throughout the fourth century aimed at prohibiting conversion to Judaism, with harsh penalties prescribed (castration for those who had themselves circumcised, exile, confiscation of property, and in some cases capital punishment).[88] Here I cite three of the numerous laws in the *Codex Theodosianus*, a major collection of Christian imperial legislation covering much of the fourth century, which seek to contain interactions between Christians and Jews. One, from 353, decreed confiscation of property for those who "become Jew from Christian and are joined to [their] sacrilegious assemblies," that is, who converted.[89] A second, dated to 383, prohibited Christians who "polluted themselves with the Jewish contagions" and forbade them from participating in Jewish worship.[90] And a third, from 388, prohibited marriages and sexual relations between Jews and Christians.[91] The fact that these laws were repeated over and again tells us two things: first, that they were ineffective; and second, that the activities cited in them were going on in the very heart of the Roman Empire, not just in distant Syria. But at the very same time, old laws were retained and new ones drafted that protected synagogues from destruction and "preserved many of the Jews' ancient privileges."[92] Speaking of the increase in anti-Jewish legislation under the Visigoths in the sixth and seventh centuries, Paula Fredriksen stresses again that even in these later centuries "we cannot move directly from the language of the law to the actual social behavior of its subjects."[93] As we will see in chapter 5, conditions in the city of Lyons, as late as the ninth century CE, when Bishop Agobard complained to the emperor, Louis the Pious, about his favorable treatment of the Jews, demonstrate the need to be mindful of the gap between rhetoric and reality and to pay careful attention to local conditions.[94]

"In death all were one." There remains one final and deeply ironic blow to the standard tale. In his survey of Jewish burial sites in Italy (Venosa, Syracuse, and Agrigento), Leonard Rutgers has noted the phenomenon of communal burial sites, involving Jews, Christians, and sometimes pagans in a single site: "Many sites from across the Roman world could be added to the list of communal Jewish-Christian-pagan cemeteries."[95] In the end, it would seem, the dead had the last word.

5

TURNING THE WORLD
UPSIDE DOWN

An Ancient Jewish Life of Jesus

The Book of the Toldos Yeshut *contains facts far more convincing*
than our gospels.

—VOLTAIRE, *L'EXAMEN IMPORTANT DE MILORD BOLINGBROKE*

I T would not be unreasonable to expect this chapter to deal with the
gospel of Matthew. It is, after all, an ancient Jewish life of Jesus, and
from many angles it seeks to turn the world upside down. Instead,
the chapter will deal with another Jewish life of Jesus, this one called the
Toledot Yeshu (*The Life of Jesus*). If the gospel of Matthew is a Jewish gospel
that is pro-Jesus, the *Toledot Yeshu* is anti-Jesus. And it has a hugely controversial history among Christians. As early as the ninth century, Latin
translations had come to the attention of the bishops of Lyons (Agobard
and his successor, Amulo). Around 1280, Ramon Marti, a Dominican friar,
produced his anti-Jewish treatise *Pugio Fidei* (*Dagger of Faith*), in which he
incorporated numerous Jewish texts, in Hebrew and Aramaic, among them
a lengthy Latin translation of the *Toledot*.[1] Marti's text then passed into
the mainstream of Christian Europe. From that time forward, the *Toledot*
circulated in Christian circles as a parade example of Jewish blasphemies

against Christianity.[2] Johannes Reuchlin (d. 1522), the distinguished Catholic humanist, fought against efforts to destroy all copies of the Talmud and other Jewish writings found among the Jews of Frankfort and Cologne. Like other Christian Hebraists of the period, Reuchlin not only studied Hebrew and read Jewish texts but supported their preservation as invaluable resources for Christian theology. But not all Jewish texts were worthy of rescue. In his *Augenspiegel* (1511), he named the *Toledot Yeshu* as a "blasphemous" text, not deserving of preservation. During the same century, various popes entered the debates over the Talmud. While no official bull mentions the *Toledot* by name, a papal brief of Pius IV (1862) mentions certain blasphemous Jewish books that probably had the *Toledot* in mind.[3] Even Jewish historians of the nineteenth and early twentieth centuries dismissed it as a tasteless fabrication in a dark corner of Jewish history and an embarrassment to Jews everywhere.

Today no one would agree with Voltaire's assessment of the *Toledot*'s historical reliability. It sheds no light whatsoever on the "historical Jesus." But it is an invaluable resource for understanding relations between Jews and Christians across many centuries. It is the earliest and most continuous witness to Jewish responses to Christian anti-Judaism in all of its forms.

There is no denying that the *Toledot* is an uncomfortable text. It is impossible to read it without a sense of embarrassment or guilt. Part of the reason for the neglect of the *Toledot* lies in the undeniable fact that it was—and still is—dangerous territory. Its many difficult moments help to explain why the *Toledot* has received so little serious attention until recent years. Before the publication of the Princeton symposium in 2011,[4] the body of serious scholarly literature consisted of Samuel Krauss's German study in 1902;[5] William Horbury's unpublished Cambridge dissertation of 1970;[6] Riccardo di Segni's important Italian book of 1985;[7] and Yaacov Deutsch's Hebrew MA thesis of 1997. Not much.

If we are to move beyond embarrassment and resentment, we need to ask the right questions. Where and when did these texts come into being? What was their purpose? And their audience? Why did Jewish communities continue to copy and circulate them across so many years, right down to the nineteenth and early twentieth centuries? What do we know about relations between Christians and Jews in Late Antiquity and the early Middle Ages (roughly the fourth to thirteenth centuries) that can help us to understand these texts? What were Christians leaders (again, mostly theologians and bishops) saying and writing about Jews and Judaism in these early centuries? These questions are absolutely essential if we are to understand these unsettling texts in their historical and cultural settings.

SOME BASIC FACTS ABOUT THE *TOLEDOT*

So far I have been speaking of the *Toledot* as if it were a single text when in fact the *Toledot* are a series of Jewish countergospels or antigospels or counterhistories, with many distinctive versions. They are not philosophical texts, such as Jews will begin to produce in the later Middle Ages, and they are not biblical commentaries, also typical of later Jewish anti-Christian polemics.[8] They are narratives, stories, tales. But they are also gospels in the sense that they follow the story line of the New Testament gospels quite closely. For the most part they begin with the accounts of Jesus's conception and birth; they proceed through his public activities, giving special emphasis to his miracles and disputes with other Jews; and they conclude with his arrest, trial, conviction, crucifixion, and burial. Like the New Testament gospels, but utterly unlike later Christian interpretations of the gospels, the *Toledot* tell a thoroughly Jewish story. All of the characters are seen as Jews—Joseph, Mary, Jesus, John the Baptist, and, most surprisingly, Peter and Paul. These characters and their story are all Jewish. Some of the characters are good guys and some are bad guys, but overall the *Toledot* insist that this is a Jewish and not a Christian tale.

Today we know of more than 170 manuscripts in libraries and archives around the Western world—in places like Cambridge University in England, the national library of Russia in St. Petersburg, and the library of the Jewish Theological Seminary in New York. Every year brings more discoveries. These manuscripts are written in a wide variety of languages. Those in Aramaic are the earliest fragments of the *Toledot*; they are just fragments but there are a good many of them. Dating from the tenth century, these Aramaic fragments are part of the enormous collection of Jewish texts found in the famous Ben Ezra synagogue in Cairo,[9] now scattered in libraries around the Western world. The largest number of manuscripts are in Hebrew and most of them are fairly late, dating from the seventeenth to the nineteenth centuries. Other languages include Judeo-Arabic (the language is Arabic but the script is Hebrew),[10] Judeo-Persian, Judeo-Spanish or Ladino, and Yiddish. Beginning in tenth-century Europe, Latin translations begin to appear in Christian circles, undoubtedly made with help from Jewish converts. Eventually the *Toledot* made their way into European vernaculars. The first German translation from Latin was produced in 1543 by Martin Luther.[11] Voltaire read them in French from one of several translations available in the eighteenth century.[12] The first printed editions of the *Toledot* were produced by Christian Hebraists in Germany—in 1681 by the anti-Jewish scholar Johan Wagenseil, complete with a full Hebrew text, a Latin translation, and copious notes, and in 1705 by Johann Huldreich, based on a totally different and unique Hebrew version.[13] In England, knowledge of the *Toledot* surfaces as early as the early seventeenth century; the first English translation appeared in the 1820s.[14]

Dating the *Toledot*, and especially their first appearance as a continuous narrative, remains a thorny issue. Estimates range from the fifth to the ninth centuries; some reach even later, some earlier. But their sources go back much further, as far back as the gospels of the New Testament, which the authors of the *Toledot* knew thoroughly and used extensively. In the mid-second century, the Christian writer Justin Martyr, in his *Dialogue with Trypho*, reports that Jews were already circulating hostile stories about Jesus:

> This Christ, who also appeared in your nation, and healed those who were maimed, and deaf, and lame in body from their birth, causing them to leap, to hear, and to see, by His word. And having raised the dead, and causing them to live, by His deeds He compelled the men who lived at that time

to recognize Him. But though they [Jews] saw such works, they asserted it was magical art. For they dared to call Him a magician, and a deceiver of the people. (69.6)

As I said before, you have sent chosen and ordained men throughout all the world to proclaim that a godless and lawless heresy had sprung from one Jesus, a Galilean deceiver, whom we [Jews] crucified; but his disciples stole him by night from the tomb, where he was laid when unfastened from the cross, and they now deceive men by asserting that he has risen from the dead and ascended to heaven. Moreover, you [Jews] accuse Him of having taught those godless, lawless, and unholy doctrines which you mention. (109).

While there is no reference here to a "published" text, Justin seems to know elements of a hostile story of Jesus that had begun to circulate among Jewish communities. Closer still to the *Toledot* are stories told by a pagan author, Celsus, in his anti-Christian treatise *The True Word*; his stories were recorded by Origen (d. 251) in his *Against Celsus*.[15] Celsus reports that he had received these stories from Jewish sources. Thus if we place Celsus close to 200 CE, his sources must date back at least to the mid-second century. And they point directly to the *Toledot*:

He [Celsus] accuses him [Jesus] of having "invented his birth from a virgin," and upbraids him with being "born in a certain Jewish village, of a poor woman of the country, who gained her subsistence by spinning, and who was turned out of doors by her husband, a carpenter by trade, because she was convicted of adultery; that after being driven away by her husband, and wandering about for a time, she disgracefully gave birth to Jesus, an illegitimate child, who having hired himself out as a servant in Egypt on account of his poverty, and having there acquired some miraculous powers, on which the Egyptians greatly pride themselves, returned to his own country, highly elated on account of them, and by means of these proclaimed himself a God." (1.28)

Let us now return to where the Jew is introduced, speaking of the mother of Jesus, and saying that "when she was pregnant she was turned out of doors by the carpenter to whom she had been betrothed, as having been guilty of adultery, and that she bore a child to a certain soldier named Panthera." (1.32)

He [Celsus] proceeds thus: "Jesus having gathered around him ten or eleven persons of notorious character, the very wickedest of tax-gatherers and sailors, fled in company with them from place to place, and obtained his living in a shameful and importunate manner." (1.62)

The Jew says, "We both found him guilty, and condemned him as deserving of death." (2.10)

Finally, toward the end of the second century, Tertullian, the first important Christian writer in Latin, had come across the following story told by Jews:

This . . . is that carpenter's son, the son of prostitution [*quasetuaria*], that Sabbath-breaker, that Samaritan and devil-possessed! This is he whom you purchased [*redemistis*] from Judas! . . . This is he whom his disciples secretly stole away, that it might be said he had risen again, or the gardener abstracted, that his lettuces might come to no harm from the crowds of visitors![16]

These early testimonies point to central themes in the *Toledot*: the virgin birth story as an attempt to cover up Mary's adultery; Jesus's flight to Egypt, where he learned magic; his return from Egypt and proclamation of himself as God; his followers as the lowest members of society; his various attempts to hide from his pursuers; his transformation of himself into a bird and his subsequent flight to Mt. Carmel, where he is finally captured; his justified condemnation to death by Jewish authorities; and (in Tertullian) the stealing of his body, somehow associated with Judas, and his burial in a garden. Whether we can conclude from these bits of reportage that there existed already in the mid-second century a full narrative, like those of the later *Toledot*, is uncertain—but possible. But that connected stories were widely circulated by that time in places as distant as North Africa (Tertullian) and Egypt (Origen) is beyond doubt.

TWO VERSIONS: ARAMAIC AND HEBREW

First, the Aramaic version(s). As mentioned above, the oldest surviving written bits of the *Toledot* are the Aramaic fragments from the Cairo Geniza.[17] In general, these Aramaic fragments reveal little overlap with the Hebrew texts. They show no birth stories, nothing about Jesus's youth or his life as a student; they lack the story of Jesus's theft of the sacred name of God from the Temple in Jerusalem and of the miracles performed with its power; and so on. On the other hand, they contain elements that do not show up in the Hebrew traditions: the leading political figure in the story is Pilate, whereas in the Hebrew texts that figure is either Herod or a mysterious Queen Helena; an elaborate story in which Jesus tries and fails to produce a child for the Roman emperor's daughter without sexual intercourse, the result of which is that she gives birth to a stone and dies; John the Baptist's role as Jesus's mentor and companion; Jesus's proclamation that both he *and John* are sons of God ("We are sons of God!");[18] and his transformation of himself into a bird. The one significant overlap between the Aramaic and the Hebrew version is the account of the trial of Jesus's disciples. But this story appears already in the Babylonian Talmud (*Sanhedrin* 43a–b). It certainly predates 500 CE and may very well have been the source for both the Aramaic and the Hebrew versions. Otherwise it shows up only in late versions of the Hebrew,[19] where it is probably the result of borrowing from one version (Aramaic) to the other (Hebrew), and in a single, unique Hebrew fragment from the Cairo Geniza.[20]

Of course it is always possible that we have found only fragments of the Aramaic *Toledot* and that it existed at some point as a much fuller narrative.

But there is good reason to suspect that the Aramaic versions really were quite different from their Hebrew cousins. When we encounter the first citations of the *Toledot* in Latin translation—in the anti-Jewish writings of Agobard and Amulo, successive bishops of Lyons in the 930s and 940s— they look very much like the Aramaic fragments.[21] Much later, in the late fourteenth century, ibn Shaprut produced his anti-Christian treatise *Eben Bohan* (*Touchstone*), in the course of which he cites two separate versions of the *Toledot*: the first, in Hebrew, follows the Hebrew versions; the second, in Aramaic, reflects the Aramaic versions. In short, while there was occasional cross-fertilization between the two traditions, they traveled for the most part on separate paths.

The Hebrew versions present an entirely different picture. If the Aramaic versions, like the gospels of Mark and John, begin in medias res, with no birth stories or accounts of Jesus's youth, the Hebrew versions follow the gospels of Matthew and Luke with their elaborate birth tales. Indeed, the Strasbourg version consciously follows and mocks the opening words of Matthew (1:1): *archê geneseos iêsou christou* (Greek)/*tehylat beryyato shel Yeshu* (Hebrew)/*beginning of the genealogy of Jesus* (*Christ*). They begin at the beginning and follow the overall structure of the gospels with striking care:

- The birth stories: Mary/Miriam is seduced by Joseph ben Pandera (in some versions it is Yochanan), a "friend" of her fiancé, Yochanan; over her strenuous protest, Joseph passes himself off as Yochanan and impregnates Mary; filled with shame, Yochanan departs for Babylonia; these stories are the *Toledot*'s counternarrative to the lengthy genealogies in Matthew and Luke, which establish Jesus's descent from David and Abraham (Matthew) and Adam (Luke).
- Jesus's education: Mary enrolls Jesus in the local yeshiva where his cleverness gets him into trouble. He disrespects his teachers and offers his own teachings (*halakhot*) in the presence of the master (a capital offense for the rabbis)—this episode is built on the story in Luke 2:41–52, where the twelve-year-old Jesus asks questions of his teachers and gives answers, to the amazement/consternation of the bystanders;[22] whereas

Luke describes Jesus's youth as a growth in wisdom, the *Toledot* sees it as a time of dramatic descent into folly.

- Jesus's power: Before approaching the central portion of Jesus's career as teacher and miracle-worker, the *Toledot* sets out to explain the source of Jesus's power—Jesus sneaks into the Temple, copies the secret name of God on a piece of parchment, stitches it into his thigh, escapes, retrieves the name, and begins his miracles; this is the *Toledot*'s countertale to the baptism stories whose goal is to establish Jesus's power as heavenly; thus there are no baptism stories in the *Toledot*.

- Debates and miracles: In response to the crowd's request for a sign/ proof of his Messianic status (Matthew 16:4 and parallels) and in reply to his fellow yeshiva students' insult that he was an illegitimate son (*mamzer*) conceived during his mother's menstrual period (*ben ha-niddah*), Jesus responds by quoting the standard biblical proof-texts from the gospels—Isaiah 7:14 ("behold a young woman / virgin will conceive and she will bear a son") and Psalm 2:7 ("You are my son, today I have begotten you")—and follows this up with miracle tales from the gospels: the healing of a leper (Mark 1:40–45) and a lame man (Mark 2:1–12); in response to his miracles, many begin to worship him; as in the New Testament gospels, Jesus's debates with his antagonists regularly take the form of biblical proof-texting; Jesus walks and rides a millstone on water (Mark 6:48); one of his followers cuts off the ear of the high priest's slave (Mark 14:47; the incident takes place later in Mark than in the *Toledot*); he claps his hands and makes mud-birds fly away.[23]

- Jesus flees: The sages (Pharisees in the gospels), worried about Jesus's large following, haul him before Queen Helena and accuse him of deceiving the people (John 7:47); no such incident appears in the gospels but the gospel of John states three times that the Jews were seeking Jesus (7:1, 11, 43), so that he flees to Galilee and hides out there in secret (7:10); the appearance before Queen Helena is the *Toledot*'s answer to the question of John 7:45, "Why did you not arrest him?" Their answer—"We did."[24]

- Jesus's struggle with Judas: The sages draft Judas Iscariot (the betrayer in the gospels; Mark 14:10–11 and parallels) to defeat Jesus, who is dazzling the crowds by flying in the air; Judas steals the sacred name and flies up to Jesus; after a struggle, Judas overcomes Jesus by urinating on him; thus polluted, both fall to the ground, their power gone.[25]

- The end: Here the pace quickens: Jesus is seized and tied to a pillar; the sages feed him vinegar (Mark 15:39 and parallels) and place a crown of thorns on his head (Mark 15:17 and parallel); but his followers manage to release him for a short stay in Antioch; finally, Jesus comes to Jerusalem at Passover (Mark 14 and parallels), is betrayed again by Judas (Mark 14:43 and parallels), put on trial with his five (!) disciples,[26] found guilty, hung up on a carob or cabbage stalk, and buried in a garden (John 19:41) or an aqueduct.

- The body: As his final act of betrayal, Judas steals the body and buries it in his garden; the disciples find the empty tomb and claim that Jesus has risen from the dead; Queen Helena scolds the sages who ask for time to discover the truth; the sages and all Israel are crestfallen until Judas reveals the true story; they recover the body, tie a rope to Jesus's legs, and drag him before Queen Helena; the sages go out in great joy.

End of story. Such is the general outline of the story in the Hebrew versions, with additions and enhancements from one text to another. Once again, it is obvious that the *Toledot* is not a single, unified text. There were no rules governing what could be included or omitted and the result is that no two manuscripts come even close to being identical. They were open texts, without fixed borders. Each community and each scribe felt free to mold the text as they saw fit in their local circumstances.[27]

Eli Yassif has stressed the literary character of the *Toledot* as folknarrative—anonymous, endlessly flexible, and belonging to no one. Yassif's standing as a folklorist also enables him to introduce two themes rarely mentioned by earlier interpreters. First, while the New Testament gospels and the *Toledot* follow the same overall pattern—the end of the main character follows from his beginning, good in the one case, bad in the other—the *Toledot* also reveal an unmistakable strand of Jewish self-criticism. Jesus's harsh treatment by his schoolmates and the rejection of his justified criticism of judges contribute to his eventual undoing but reflect badly on his critics. And the aerial battle of Jesus and Judas reveals, and helps to define, "the thin line between the pure and the impure in ancient Judaism."[28] Jesus is an unwitting victim in this process. The second theme highlights an unmistakable feature of all versions of the Hebrew *Toledot*—their setting in a yeshiva, the schoolhouse, or *bet midrash*. Jesus's early companions are his fellow yeshiva students and his later antagonists are the sages, or rabbis in these schools. All of this points, for Yassif, to "the world of *yeshiva* students in Jewish Babylonia in the eighth century" as the most likely setting for the circulation, if not the origin, of these stories.[29]

A HYBRID VERSION: FIRKOVICH

No manuscript better illustrates the "mixed" character of the *Toledot* than the so-called Firkovich text, edited and interpreted by Yaacov Deutsch.[30] For this reason alone, it is worth a brief detour. The Firkovich manuscript stands as a kind of bridge between the earlier Aramaic fragments and the later Hebrew manuscripts. Abraham Firkovich himself (d. 1874), a wealthy Karaite and world-traveler, collected huge numbers of ancient manuscripts, including some from the Cairo Geniza and others from the geniza of the nearby Karaite synagogue. After his death, his enormous collection was sold by his family to the Russian National Library in St. Petersburg, where it marks one of the great collections of Judaica (along with Samaritan and Karaite materials) in the world.

The manuscript dates itself precisely to 1536. It is a full gospel, beginning with a birth story and ending with Jesus's death and burial. What is peculiar about the Firkovich manuscript is that it has been translated from an Aramaic original.[31] Though written in Hebrew, it contains numerous Aramaic words, sentences, phrases, and occasional places where the translator simply misunderstood the Aramaic original. But unlike the Aramaic fragments from the Cairo Geniza, it also includes a birth narrative, although it is not clear that this part of the text stems from the Aramaic source. In other words, the Firkovich text represents a hybrid of the two traditions—in fact, so far as we know, it is the only one of its kind. Thus, while the Aramaic and Hebrew versions tended to follow separate paths, there were occasional crossovers.

TWO EPISODES: JESUS'S BIRTH AND BURIAL

Just as in the New Testament (or at least in Matthew and Luke), the story begins with Mary's pregnancy and Jesus's birth. But before we look at what the *Toledot* do with these stories, we need to remind ourselves of what the New Testament gospels themselves say about them. First of all, Mark has no birth narrative at all and Joseph is never mentioned. Jesus is referred to once as the son of Mary. This is peculiar. It was extraordinarily rare in the ancient Mediterranean to refer to anyone with reference to the mother. From a purely literary perspective, then, we would have to call Joseph an absentee father. The gospel of John, which also lacks a birth story, presents an even more paradoxical picture of the family. On the one hand, Jesus's father is repeatedly identified as his Father in heaven, that is, God; on the other hand, and *only in John*, Joseph is twice mentioned as Jesus's father, once in 1:45 and again in 6:42. This muddled picture seems to have led to, or perhaps to have stemmed from, uncertainties about Jesus's paternity. Elsewhere, in John 8, as part of an angry exchange between Jesus and the *ioudaioi* (Judeans), we find a strained debate about paternity. "Where is your father?" demand the *ioudaioi* (Jn 8:19). A reasonable question given Joseph's overall absence in the story. In the same chapter, the Judeans deny that they are illegitimate offspring and claim Abraham as their (fore)father. And just before this debate, we find the story of the woman taken in adultery (8:1–11). In other words, it looks as though the author of John's gospel, already in the first century CE, is struggling with accusations of adultery and illegitimacy directed at Jesus. At an early date, the question of Jesus's paternity had become an issue not just for outsiders but for believers as well.

When we turn to Matthew and Luke, we find two elaborate and totally different birth stories. Matthew 1:18–19 begins the story: "Now the birth of Jesus took place in this way. When his mother was engaged to Joseph, but before they lived together, she was found to be with child—from the Holy Spirit. Her husband Joseph, being a righteous man [= pious Jew] and unwilling to expose her to public disgrace, planned to dismiss her/send her away." The passage goes on to tell the story of the angel who appears to reassure Joseph that everything is OK and that her child is—same expression—"from the Holy Spirit."[32] As we know from later Christian history, this story eventually became the foundation of the doctrine of the Virgin Birth, which stands as one of the pillars in Christian theology and piety. It is a fundamental building block of the view that Jesus is none other than the divine son of God. But underlying the narrative in Matthew—just as in John—there appears to be a concern about the joint issues of illegitimacy and adultery. There is, I think, no other way to interpret Joseph's reaction to Mary's pregnancy than to see it as suspicion of adultery. Joseph knows that he is not the father and he clearly suspects someone else.

Now, what do the *Toledot* do with their version of these issues? First of all, they clearly take their point of departure from the story in Matthew, where illegitimacy and adultery are already part of the picture. Into this story, the *Toledot* introduce two new characters—or rather they fill in two gaps in the story. The two characters are Joseph Pandera and Yochanan. Of course, neither of these is really new. Joseph Pandera is the Joseph of the New Testament gospels, the same Pandera named by Celsus around 150 CE and in Rabbinic sources some 250 years later. But here he has acquired the additional name of Pandera. The origins of the name are not clear. Some have proposed that it represents a mocking anagram of the Greek word for virgin, *parthenos*. Others have pointed to the gravestone of a Roman soldier from Bingerbrück in Germany and have recalled Celsus's comment that Jesus was the son of a soldier (presumably Roman) whose name was Panthera. On the gravestone, the soldier's name is given as Tiberius Julius Abdes Pantera of Sidon (a city on the coast, north of the present-day border between Israel and Lebanon); his military service is noted as a former standard-bearer of the first cohort of archers (*exs coh[orte] I sagittariorum*), a unit known to have served in Roman Palestine during the early decades of the first century CE. Did this historical Pantera have anything to do with our story?

Impossible to tell. But it did generate one of the most amusing remarks in all of modern scholarship. Speculating about some sort of connection, Morton Smith once wrote: "It is possible, though not likely, that his tombstone from Bingerbrück is our only genuine relic of the Holy Family."[33]

As for Yochanan, I have no doubt that he is based on the figure of John the Baptist, Jesus's companion, mentor, and rival in the gospels. But here is where the inversion of the New Testament gospel stories begins. In most versions of the *Toledot*, Mary's fiancé is Yochanan, not Joseph. Yochanan/John is the good guy, the pious Jew, deceived and betrayed by his cunning buddy Joseph. Joseph is the bad guy. He is an oversexed lecher who falls in love with Mary and lusts after her. He sets out to seduce her. In the simplest versions of this story, a drunken Joseph slips into Mary's house one stormy night, pretends to be her pious fiancé, and over her vigorous protests—she cries out that she is in her menstrual period and thus off limits—sleeps with her. Mary becomes pregnant. When Yochanan learns of what has happened, he flees to Babylonia, where he becomes a respected sage. In more elaborate versions of the story, Joseph collaborates with his mother to stage a formal banquet for their extended family—and Mary. After a number of twists and turns, again over Mary's protests and again pretending to be Yochanan, Joseph seduces Mary and makes her pregnant with Jesus.

As scandalous as these transformations of the Christian story may seem to us, and certainly seemed to many Christian readers in Late Antiquity, the Middles Ages, and beyond, we need to make two points. First, the *Toledot* version derives directly from the text of Matthew, where Joseph suspects Mary of adultery. In other words, they are exploiting what I would call a hole in the gospel story, a hole unmistakably visible not just in Matthew but in John as well. And for all of its inversions, the *Toledot* keep one thing constant—just as in the gospel of John, Jesus's father is Joseph. Against those who see the *Toledot* as made of pure fabrications, we need to remind ourselves that for all of their inversions, the basic structure of the story comes straight out of the New Testament gospels. Second, the *Toledot* here are attacking Christian claims about Jesus at their very foundation. No, they say, Jesus is not the divine son of God, conceived by divine intervention. He is the illegitimate son of Mary and a drunken neighbor who deceived his friend and seduced his fiancée. This is the Jewish response to Christian anti-Judaism.

A similar pattern emerges when we turn to the second episode, at the end of the story—the question of what happened to Jesus's body. Once again we need to look first at what the New Testament gospels say about the end of Jesus's life. The most intriguing version, also the earliest, is the gospel of Mark. Mary Magdalene and another Mary go to Jesus's tomb and find his body missing. A mysterious figure informs them that he had been raised or taken up. The Greek verb is ἠγέρθη/*êgerthê* and it is not entirely clear what it means here. Much later it will be interpreted as meaning "he was resurrected from the dead," but here it could just as well mean that he had simply been "lifted up and taken away." What favors this reading, I think, is the reaction of the women. They are not reassured by the stranger's words. They run from the tomb in terror and dismay: "they said nothing to anyone, for they were afraid" (16:8). The text does not say what they were afraid of, but it is not too much to suggest that the issue was the missing body of Jesus. What had happened to it? Where was it? Who had lifted it up and taken it away?

The gospels of Matthew and Luke also record the story of the empty tomb, but they convert the women's fear in Mark into an account of Jesus's miraculous resurrection from the dead. Fear and trembling have been eliminated. But Matthew—here again Matthew plays a special role for the *Toledot*—adds an element that is missing from the other gospels. After Jesus's death and burial, the chief priests and Pharisees approach the Roman governor Pilate with this startling demand:

> My Lord, we remember what that impostor said while he was still alive. "After three days I will rise again." Therefore command the tomb to be made secure until the third day; otherwise his disciples will go and steal him away and tell the people, "He has been raised from the dead."[34] Pilate said to them, "You have a guard of soldiers; go and make it as secure as you can." So they went with the guard and made the tomb secure by sealing the stone.

In the next chapter (28:11–15) the same theme appears again. The guards fear for their lives when the tomb is discovered to be empty; the chief priests advise them to make up a story about what happened:

> This is what you should say, "His disciples came at night and stole him away while we were asleep. And if this story comes to the governor's ears we will reassure him and keep you out of trouble."

At the end of this passage a later editor adds his own conclusion: "and this story is told among the Jews until this very day."

In other words, even before the gospel of Matthew was written down, that is, thirty-five to forty years after the death of Jesus, Jewish critics had their own version of why the tomb was empty. And decades, or even centuries, later, the *Toledot* tell a similar tale. Once again, the *Toledot* exploit a hole in the account of the gospels—the hole being uncertainty about what happened to Jesus's body. But in their version, it is not the disciples who steal the body. There it is the familiar figure of Judas—the disloyal follower of Jesus in the New Testament gospels—who beats them to it. Fearing that the disciples would steal the body and claim that Jesus had been raised from the dead, Judas steals the body himself, buries it in a water channel in his garden, and later shows it to the authorities to prove that there was no miraculous resurrection. The point here, just to state the obvious, is to show that Jesus's predictions of his resurrection and the disciples' belief in it were nothing but empty boasts and lies.[35] Christianity has no legitimacy.

Once again, in this second episode, we learn that the *Toledot Yeshu* are all about an effort to dismantle the second major pillar in Christian beliefs about the figure of Jesus, where his resurrection from the dead guaranteed his status as divine redeemer and son of God. For the authors of the *Toledot*, Jesus was neither the divine redeemer nor the son of God, and the proof was to be found in the Christian gospels themselves. Their goal was to delegitimize Christian beliefs and Christian authority. The truth lay not with those who were persecuting the Jews but with the Jews themselves.

THE ACTS OF THE APOSTLES:
PART 2 OF THE *TOLEDOT*

In numerous versions of the *Toledot* (but not in the Aramaic fragments), the narrative extends beyond the life of Jesus to include accounts of what happened after his death—much like the Book of Acts, which follows immediately after the gospels in the Christian New Testament. These stories are what I call part 2 of the *Toledot*. And it comes as no surprise that the two main characters in this extended story are Peter and Paul, just as in the Book of Acts.

These stories are truly amazing. Let me describe briefly what happens to Peter. First, we need to remind ourselves of who we are dealing with. In the official Christian version of history, Peter is the immediate successor to Jesus, the first Christian pope, and the first Christian martyr in Rome. In the Jewish versions of history, Peter undergoes a complete transformation. He becomes a subversive double agent, a pretend Christian, commissioned by the Jewish sages to undermine Christianity by delivering false instructions in Rome. Far from being a pious Christian, he lives his entire life as an observant Jew, isolated in his special tower. One day a year, he emerges to deliver false teachings of his own making, the most important of which is that Christians should leave Jews in peace and stop persecuting them. For the remaining 364 days of the year, Peter sits alone in his tower, eating no unclean food, composing liturgical poems (*piyyutim*) for use in synagogues throughout the Jewish world. In a number of medieval Jewish texts outside the *Toledot* but probably influenced by them, under the name of Shimon Kefa (the name of Peter in the New Testament gospels) he is credited with having composed the Nishmat prayer, still part of the synagogue liturgy for the Sabbath and Passover, as well as basic elements of the Yom Kippur liturgy. So famous did he become among Jews of later generations that the date of his death became a regular day of commemoration in the Jewish calendar. In a word, Peter became a great hero of the Jews, nothing less than a kind of messiah, who saved the Jews from Christian persecution.[36]

Paul plays a similar role in a number of versions:

- In the Strasbourg manuscript, Eliahu/Elijah calls himself an apostle of Jesus and urges Christians to separate themselves from Jews and to abandon Jewish practices. At the end of this section, the text reads, "This Eliahu showed them all the (Christian) laws that are not good and he did this for the healing of Israel and the Christians call him Paulos; after Paulos gave them these laws and commandments, the fools separated themselves from Israel and the disputes disappeared."[37] Here Elijah, the prophet of Israel, and Paul are identified as cosaviors of the Jews.

- In the Vienna manuscript, Paul is again identified with Elijah, whose features are entirely Pauline. He is summoned by the sages and performs miracles to convince the followers of Jesus of his apostolic status: "And he said, 'The main thing that Jesus wants from you is that you separate yourselves from the Jews in teaching, in language, in meetings in Sabbaths, and in festivals and that you make your own prayer houses.' And they all answered and said, 'Just as you said, we will do.' And from then on they separated from the Jews and did everything he commanded of them and they asked his name and he said, 'S. PAULO.' And the disciples went their way and the evil ones went their way/separated from being Jews and the world was peaceful and they made a dwelling for S. Paulo so that he would live there and not be polluted by food or drink."[38]

- In the relatively late Tam u-Muad version, Paul, also called Abba Shaul (= Saul), preaches the abandonment of circumcision and the establishment of new Christian festivals. As a result of his efforts to protect the Jews, he earned a good name for himself among the sages. "He also gained a place in the world to come together with Rabbi Yochanan/John the Baptist. For through their wisdom they were a shelter and a refuge for Israel. They rebuilt the ruins that the Christians had destroyed in Israel."[39]

In summing up the significance of these passages, Samuel Krauss concludes that Paul has been given a messianic role, as the savior of Israel, much like Peter, the prophet Elijah, and Yochanan/John the Baptist.[40] This image will enjoy a long afterlife well beyond its Jewish origins. The Muslim author ibn Ḥazam (d. 1064) wrote that "the Jews bribed the Benjamite Paul to have him mislead the followers of Jesus, by teaching them that Jesus was God."[41] The image of Paul as a loyal Jew was alive and well in Jewish and Muslim circles for more than a millennium and a half before it was (re) discovered in the late twentieth century by Jewish and Christian scholars.

THE *TOLEDOT* AND THE POGROM
IN VIENNA, 1420–1421

As a final word, let me lay out an anecdote from the end of the Middle Ages. In the 1450s, the Austrian priest and scholar Thomas Ebendorfer produced the first complete translation of the *Toledot* into Latin, with help from a Jewish convert. The question is, why then? What would have brought the Hebrew *Toledot* to Ebendorfer's attention at that particular moment in Austrian history? Ebendorfer himself provides the answer. In one of his anti-Jewish writings, he reports that in 1420 local Christians had accused a Jewish woman of stealing elements of the Christian Eucharist from a local church and subjecting them to mockery. In this period and for a long time after, these accusations—of what was known as host-desecrations—circulated widely in Western Christianity.[42] These charges often led to persecution and murder. In our case, the consequences in Vienna were serious indeed. Jewish property was confiscated; Jews were imprisoned; and many died under miserable conditions during a harsh winter. Some Jews underwent last-minute conversions, while others committed suicide rather than submit. In the end, the remaining Jews of the city were put to death by fire. Shortly thereafter, Duke Albrecht VI of Austria banished all Jews from the land of Austria. The Jews of Vienna and Austria experienced a violent and full-blown pogrom. The Jewish community in Vienna was all but eradicated.

What interests us here is the fact that the *Toledot* were copied and circulated in at least one local Jewish community at this time and that references to it show up in a contemporary account of these events. One of these reports speaks of certain insulting (*execrabilis*) Jewish books in the possession of local Jews. The *Toledot*, well known to Ebendorfer, must have been one of these books. How would they have come to the attention of the Christian authorities, among them Thomas Ebendorfer? Through Jewish converts eager to show their loyalty to their new faith.[43] There is little doubt that the *Toledot* circulated among Jews precisely at the time of the pogrom. In fact, a marginal note in Ebendorfer's Latin translation of the *Toledot* makes a specific reference to the pogrom in Vienna.[44] In his introduction to the translation, Ebendorfer describes the physical *Toledot* and, more importantly, its use: "I determined that there was a little book, kept secret,[45] that they open time and again with great enthusiasm and shove it before their children from an early age; and they are prepared, even on the holiest night of the year and also on the birthday of our Lord and Savior to recite in a public gathering the shameful things, with great interest and attention."[46] This is a sad and tragic story. Its details are preserved in a Jewish document, the *Wiener Gesera*, composed by an eyewitness of these events and by Ebendorfer himself in his *Cronica Austrie*, written in 1450.[47] But for us it is also a revealing story. It offers a vivid picture of the circumstances in which the *Toledot Yeshu* provided answers to urgent questions: "How could these things happen to us?" "Who is doing these things?"

CONCLUSIONS, OR WHAT THE *TOLEDOT YESHU* TELL US

Against the old view—a view that is still around in some scholarly circles—that Jews did not know much about Christianity and did not care much either, the many versions of the *Toledot*, along with the passages from Origen and Tertullian, show just the opposite. Not only were the authors of the *Toledot* thoroughly familiar with the New Testament, but they show knowledge of later Christian literature as well.[48] From the very beginning Jews were concerned to refute claims about Jesus.[49] He and his movement were disruptive. In the New Testament gospels, replete with charges against him, this was an entirely inner-Jewish affair—one Jewish group against another. But as Christianity expanded and began to express increasingly hostile views of Jews and Judaism, the debate ceased being an intramural affair and took on more ominous tones. From the mid-fourth century onward, when Christianity became allied with the Roman state, Christian anti-Judaism began to have social, political, legal, and economic consequences. Later still, from the ninth century onward, Christian anti-Judaism and its sibling, anti-Semitism, posed serious existential threats to Jewish communities in Europe. A Jewish response became urgent and the *Toledot* played a central role in that drama. This is not to say that Jews were subjected to harsh treatment at all times and in every place. But at some times and in some places it was so. Efforts to convert Jews took on greater energy beginning in the eighth century. And at all times, Jews felt the pressure of a dominant Christian culture.

The intended original audience of the *Toledot* was an internal Jewish one. They were never meant to be read by outsiders, for Jews feared that their contents could only offend their Christian neighbors. They were written in Hebrew, Aramaic, and other Jewish languages, all of which were inaccessible to virtually all Christian readers. What we see is Jews speaking to themselves, pushing back against a Christian anti-Judaism that surrounded them on all sides: in anti-Jewish writings, in the destruction of synagogues, in anti-Jewish imperial and ecclesiastical legislation, and later in the Crusades and Inquisitions. What this tells us is that the ancient and continuous expressions of Christian anti-Judaism did have a serious impact on Jewish communities. They felt the sting. And they needed to respond, not so much to Christians but rather to members of their own communities who experienced anxiety, doubt, and pressure as victims of Christian persecution and debasement, as targets of efforts to convert Jews, and as anxious minorities. Thus one fundamental role of the *Toledot* was to alleviate that anxiety, to resolve that doubt, and to resist that cultural pressure. This is what makes the *Toledot* uncomfortable reading.

One particular feature of the *Toledot* that has never drawn the attention that it deserves is the recurrent theme of Jewish conversions to Christianity.[50] In many versions of the *Toledot* the theme is prominent: Jews, especially young Jews, were embracing the alien religion. We know of few such cases before the thirteenth century, but after that and especially during the

Crusades and later the Inquisitions, conversions and pseudoconversions became more numerous and more worrisome. They demanded a response, for such conversions certainly raised doubts in Jewish communities, especially when converts turned against their former faith with anti-Jewish polemics.[51] So it was with prominent figures like Nicholas Donin, who played a central role in the Paris trial of the Talmud in 1240; Pablo Christiani, who debated against Ramban/Nachmanides in the famous Barcelona debates of 1263; and Abner of Burgos (d. 1348), the former Alfonso do Valladolid, who produced numerous polemical and apologetic works after his conversion. These were significant and well-educated figures who had turned their Jewish learning against their former faith. Jews must have asked, "What does this say about our faith if such Jews embrace those who treat us so mercilessly?" In these settings, the function of the *Toledot* was to eliminate these doubts and to strengthen Jewish communities whose faith must have been shaken by conversions to Christianity. And in some cases it was to win back Jewish converts.[52]

The goal of this chapter has been to demonstrate that the *Toledot Yeshu* amount to anything but, as one critic put it, "instructive evidence of a *regrettable popular psychosis*."[53] On the contrary, in the *Toledot*, Jewish communities produced their own version of the beliefs and practices of the religion that stood against them. These counternarratives made it possible for them to hold fast to their own faith under the most trying circumstances. However much they suffered, they could feel reassured that truth and justice were on their side. Not only was Christianity a false religion, devoid of all truth, it was a Jewish creation, produced by two Jewish heroes, Peter and Paul.

6

EPILOGUE

I have often asked myself the question, "Does any of this really matter?" What difference does it make that the "new" Paul was a Jew; that there was no Christianity, or even any idea of Christianity in his time; or that, to choose but one example, the gospel of Matthew is a text not just influenced by Judaism but a Jewish text? Does anyone really care that there was no centuries-long Jewish polemic against Paul, not until the nineteenth century, and that instead we find Paul treated as a loyal and observant Jew who defended his fellow Jews against a hostile Christianity? So what that Jewish communities and synagogues did not disappear from the scene with the birth of Christianity, as traditional views would have it, or that significant numbers of non-Jews—Gentiles and Christians—found their way to synagogues and were welcomed there by local Jews? And does it really matter—today—that Jews did not wither away under the onslaught of Christian anti-Judaism and anti-Semitism in Late Antiquity and the early Middle Ages? And what about those we call Jewish Christians, who worshiped Jesus and observed the Jewish Law? Emerging mainstream Christians sought to write them out of their history. But did they really matter then, or now? Is all of this just so much academic bloviation? In short, who cares?

Scholars certainly care. The mountain of writing about Paul proves that. But with decidedly mixed results. Scholarship is about pursuit of the truth. Do your claims match the evidence? Have you read your texts—in whatever form—without prejudice? Does your interpretation of the text make sense in the times and circumstances when they were first written? Do your arguments hold up to close examination? Have you considered all the available sources? Is what you say about them true?

Here it must be said, as numerous recent critics have argued, that most traditional Christian interpreters fail these texts. Their readings are anachronistic. They read back into Paul views that emerged long after his time, most notably, the very idea of Christianity and with it Christian anti-Judaism. G. F. Moore and Charlotte Klein, among others, have demonstrated with great vigor that Christian views of Paul and Judaism are deeply rooted in Christian theology. Moore's judgment, cited in chapter 4, is worth repeating here: "Christian interest in Jewish literature has always been apologetic or polemic rather than historical." Thus, against the plain meaning of his letters, Paul becomes a Christian and the maker of anti-Judaism. Along with this anachronistic reading come, as E. P. Sanders and others have shown, a woeful ignorance and distortion of the Judaism in which Paul—not to mention Jesus, Matthew, the author of the Apocalypse, and numerous others—was deeply embedded. Despite claims that they were returning to the original Jewish sources in their efforts to understand Paul's Judaism, it is hard to avoid Sander's conclusion: "one cannot avoid the suspicion that in fact, Paul's own polemic against Judaism serves to define the Judaism which is then contrasted [unfavorably, of course] with Paul's thought."[1] All too often, Christian exegetes have misread what Paul says about Jews and Judaism and then turned around to use that distorted image in their descriptions of Judaism "as it really was."

The consequences of these anachronistic readings of Paul are as numerous as they are fatal. First, as Sanders notes, Jewish scholars (and Sanders too) have been absorbed in "the 'wearying struggle' to get Christian scholars to see Rabbinic Judaism (or Pharisaism) in an unbiased light."[2] It is wearying because their efforts seem to have so little effect. We need to understand why these efforts have encountered such stubborn resistance.

Second, the Paul who emerges from this scholarship "comes out of no-where."[3] As Stowers states repeatedly, the Paul of Christian exegesis "makes no sense for a Jew in Paul's era . . . The more we have learned about Judaism as it actually existed rather than the Judaism of Christian imagination, the more impossible it has become to give a historical account of the tradi-tional Paul."[4] Yet another consequence is the realization that translations, commentaries, dictionaries, and the like are themselves deeply permeated by traditional anti-Jewish assumptions. As Lloyd Gaston has noted, "It's almost paralyzing when it comes to writing, for so little can be assumed and all must be discussed."[5] One thing is clear. Once the distorted view of Judaism is cast aside, the old Paul and its supportive apparatus go with it.

The picture painted by Moore, Klein, Sanders, Gaston, and Stowers is bleak indeed. Towering figures of modern scholarship are indicted. Still, the distorted view of Judaism—and with it the old Paul—has shown re-markable persistence. But these authors are themselves proof that Moore's law about Christian views of Judaism—that Christian interest in Jewish literature has always been apologetic or polemical rather than historical—can be broken. And when it is, new truths come to the fore: Paul was not a Christian or the maker of Christian anti-Judaism; he is a first-century Jew who makes sense only in that setting; the gospel of Matthew is a thor-oughly Jewish text; and so on. And along with these new truths, the old views prove to be untenable. All of this matters to scholars, if to no one else. Scholarship is about the pursuit of truth. How can we get it right? How can we know when we do?

Why should all of this matter to Jews? I can hardly speak for Jews—or for Christians—but I can report that Paul has mattered among Jews, not just in the present but for many centuries. His absence from rabbinic litera-ture is intriguing. There may be hints and traces here and there in Rabbinic literature but overall the absence is striking. What to make of it? Does it amount to condemnation by silence? Perhaps. But this is far from certain. We may come closer if we heed Eli Yassif's observation that the early ver-sions of the *Toledot Yeshu* probably emerged among students of the rabbis in the yeshivas of Babylon. Here it may be useful to recall that Jesus's story in the *Toledot* is set among yeshiva students and that his teachers are known

Jewish sages.[6] Moreover, Michael Sokoloff has shown that the language of the earliest Aramaic fragments reflects the language of Babylonian Jewish literature generally, including the Talmud. And while the episodes surrounding Paul (and Peter) do not appear at all in the Aramaic fragments, it is not too much to speculate—but it is only speculation—that oral stories about the two apostles circulated in those same circles and emerged in written form only at a later date.

In any case, once and whenever the cycle of stories about Paul and Peter did emerge, what we find is a complete appropriation of the apostle as a loyal, observant Jew and much more. He becomes something like a savior figure by rescuing Jews from Christian persecution and urging Christians to separate themselves entirely from Jews and Judaism. From that point on, reaching through Profiat Duran, Spinoza, and Jacob Emden, with a brief detour beginning in the nineteenth century in figures like Graetz and Klausner, Paul becomes not just a central but even a positive figure in Jewish thought. Graetz and Klausner, for whom Paul was central but negative, begin to look like momentary hiccups in the *longue durée* of Jewish Pauls. Even a partial list of modern Jewish writers who have recovered a Jewish Paul is impressive: Asch, Flusser, Ben Chorin, Buber, Taubes, Wyschogrod, Boyarin, Eisenbaum, Lapide, Nanos, and, more recently, Ishay Rosen-Zvi and his students at Tel Aviv University. At the conclusion of his study on the Jewish "Heimholung" (Recovery) of Paul, Stefan Meissner can state that most Jewish readers of Paul today insist that Paul was not a convert from Judaism to Christianity and that he remained a Jew to the end.[7] Only as a Jew does he make sense. And if we expand the horizon to include studies of the gospels (not to mention the figure of Jesus), we could add the names of Kister and Furstenberg.

But why has the apostle mattered so much to Jews from the fourth century to the present? Michael Wyschogrod has offered compelling answers to this question. His Jewish Paul, the one who neither converted to Christianity nor repudiated Judaism, leads him to speak of a post-supersessionist Christianity that will "sense the overwhelming love with which God relates to his people [the Jews] and find it possible to participate in that love."[8] Gentile Christians will understand themselves as "the gathering of people around the people of Israel . . . Through the Jew Jesus, when properly understood, the gentile enters into the covenant and becomes a member of the household, *as long as he or she does not claim that his or her entrance replaces the original children.*"9 This is presumably what Wyschogrod means in his confession "that it is difficult for me to see how a thinking orthodox Jew can avoid coping with the Paul-and-Luther criticism of the law."10 So this is why Paul matters to Wyschogrod. Pauline Christians will view themselves as adopted children of the household, alongside the Jews as God's permanently beloved people, and Jews, for their part, will recognize Pauline Christians as new members of the same household. Wyschogrod's Jewish Paul lays heavy consequences on both parties. As for Wyschogrod himself, it is clear that his engagement with Paul has "helped [him] shape a Jewish identity that can live in deep appreciation of this new [Pauline] Christianity."11 Implicit in Wyschogrod's views, and presumably in those of other Jewish proponents of the "new" Paul, is the further claim that any form of Christian anti-Judaism or supersessionism is un-Pauline, un-Biblical, and thus un-Christian.

In a review of my earlier work *The Origins of Anti-Semitism: Attitudes Toward Judaism in Pagan and Christian Antiquity,*12 a reviewer, in a generally positive assessment, comments that in order to substantiate my claims about Paul, Gager "would have to claim that Paul considers Jews still *obliged* to maintain the Torah, that Jews who do become followers of Christ are nevertheless forbidden to escape the Torah commandments in any way. Even Gager cannot extend his reading of Paul that far; he does not even try."13 Let me try now. Here is a case where these chapters matter. Paul himself was Jew who followed Christ and (nevertheless) still observed the Torah commandments. About this there is now general agreement. Augustine affirmed that this behavior was fully justified for Paul and presumably for other Jesus-worshiping Jews. In the Book of Acts, Paul (16:3) had his Jewish coworker circumcised. His arguments against observance apply only to Gentile Jesus-worshipers. Much later, Profiat Duran, Jacob Emden, and the *Toledot Yeshu* make the same point. Paul insisted that Jews are obligated to observe the Torah, as he did himself; only Gentiles are released from that obligation. Paul was not alone among Jesus-worshiping Jews who observed the commandments. As we have seen, this is an adequate description of early (and later) Jewish Christians. For them, observance was not an option but an obligation. Of course, they believed that Paul forbade Jews who worshiped Jesus to follow the commandments. But here they certainly misunderstood the apostle.

After reading Wyschogrod, the question of why the Jewish Paul matters to Christians should have become evident. Lloyd Gaston has put the issue in the starkest possible terms: "A Christian Church with an anti-Semitic New Testament is abominable, but a Christian Church without a New Testament is inconceivable . . . A New Testament without . . . the Pauline corpus as its formal center would not be the New Testament at all." In short, traditional readings of Paul, Matthew, Mark, and the Apocalypse lead, and have led, to an illegitimate Christianity, an unacceptable New Testament. Unless some other reading can be reached, Christianity itself must be abandoned. Some have said that Gaston's discovery of the Jewish Paul amounts to little more than wishful thinking, a failed attempt to rescue his faith from the pit of anti-Judaism. In fact, Gaston's faith functioned as motivation, not excuse. It released him from the strictures of traditional thinking. And he has been joined by many others, Jews and non-Christians, for whom preserving Christianity is not an issue.

There can be little doubt that the discovery of the Jewish Paul, along with the Jewish gospels and the Jewish Jesus, has had a real impact on the thinking of various Christian churches and denominations. The publication of *Nostra Aetate*, by the Roman Catholic Church at Vatican II in 1965, specifically repudiated anti-Judaism and declared that God's covenant with Israel remains fully valid and intact. Pope John Paul II, who presided over Vatican II, declared in a sermon that God's covenant with the Jewish people was irrevocable. Among mainline American Protestant groups, the Presbyterian Church (USA), the United Church of Christ, and the United Methodist Church have repudiated all forms of anti-Judaism and supersessionism and have rejected the traditional claim that the divine covenant with the Jews has been invalidated by the advent of Jesus. And various evangelical churches have similarly embraced the view that Jews remain

God's chosen people.[14] As a result, in all of these cases, efforts to convert Jews have been largely abandoned. There is no point. Jews are already "in."

And what about modern anti-Semitism? Does the new Paul matter there? This is not the place to examine modern anti-Semitism in all of its dimensions. There is no straightforward, monocausal line that leads from anti-Judaism to modern anti-Semitism. Modern anti-Semitism is a highly complex phenomenon, with roots in politics, pseudoscience, and racial prejudice. But there is no denying, as many have argued, that without anti-Judaism anti-Semitism could not have arisen. If anti-Judaism is removed from post-supersessionist Christianity, one of the main pillars of anti-Semitism will have been removed.

So this stuff does matter. So far, I have concentrated pretty much on the Jewish Paul. What about other threads of the story, say, the role of synagogues as gathering places for Jews and others in the early centuries of the Common Era? Nothing even remotely like this has existed since that time: synagogues where up to half of the congregants, especially on the great holidays, would have consisted of non-Jews, pagans and Christians. Here the relevance for today is less obvious. The point is not to say that contemporary synagogues should revert to that model, even if they could. Instead, we need to understand that good history is like a travelogue. It releases us from our present, limited conditions, if only in our imagination. It enhances and expands our vision. It offers us new possibilities for thinking and being.

NOTES

INTRODUCTION

1. Horace, *Epistles*, 2.1.156: "Captive Greece held captive her uncouth conqueror and brought the arts to the rustic Latin lands."

2. On the issue of martyrdom, see D. Boyarin, *Dying for God: Martyrdom and the Making of Christianity and Judaism* (Stanford: Stanford University Press, 1999); G. W. Bowersock, *Martyrdom and Rome* (New York: Cambridge University Press, 2002); and E. Castelli, *Martyrdom and Memory: Early Christian Culture Making* (New York: Columbia University Press, 2004).

3. Ignatius, *Magnesians*, 8.1 and 10.2.

4. See the extensive discussion by S. Cohen, "Ioudaïzein, 'to Judaize,'" in *The Beginnings of Jewishness: Boundaries, Varieties, Uncertainties* (Berkeley: University of California Press, 1999).

5. Ignatius, *Philadelphians*, 4.

6. Ignatius, *Philadelphians*, 6.

7. The phrase "conceptual nihilation" belongs to T. Luckmann and P. Berger, *The Social Construction of Reality: A Treatise in the Sociology of Knowledge* (Garden City, N.Y.: Doubleday, 1966), 159–160.

8. Jonathan Elukin has argued—in *Living Together, Living Apart: Rethinking Jewish-Christian Relations in the Middle Ages* (Princeton: Princeton

University Press, 2007)—that historians have overplayed the role of conflict and tension between Christians and Jews and that we should instead see the norm as one in which Jews and Christians lived together in relative peace. In challenging this lachrymose view of Jewish history, he argues that periods of hostility and violence were the exception, not the norm. David Nierenberg adopts a different view. Once established, the vocabularies of hatred represented the constant potential for violence. He questions "the very existence of an age of peaceful and idyllic *convivencia*, whether long or short." Nierenberg, *Communities of Violence: Persecution of Minorities in the Middle Ages* (Princeton: Princeton University Press, 1996), 9.

9. See P. Richardson, "The Beginnings of Christian Anti-Judaism," in *The Cambridge History of Judaism*, vol. 4, ed. S. T. Katz (Cambridge: Cambridge University Press, 2006), 244–258; and P. Fredriksen and O. Irshai, "Christian Anti-Judaism: Polemics and Policies," in Katz, *The Cambridge History of Judaism*, 977–1034.

10. A notable exception to this pattern appears in efforts by some political and church leaders to protect Jews during the Crusades. See the discussion on the First Crusade (1096) in R. Chazan, "The Pattern of the Response," in *European Jewry and the First Crusade* (Berkeley: University of California Press, 1987).

11. M. Simon, *Verus Israel: A Study of the Relations Between Christians and Jews in the Roman Empire, 135–425* (New York: Oxford University Press, 1986), 140.

12. Such was the case in Carthage during the time of Tertullian. In his *Against the Jews*, he reports a public debate, complete with vocal supporters on both sides, that lasted a full day. What irritated Tertullian more than anything else was that the Jewish debater was a Gentile convert.

13. So in the debate between Justin Martyr and his Jewish collocutor Trypho. Of course, Justin's long-winded account in his *Dialogue with Trypho* is anything but a transcript of what really took place.

14. On the tradition of Philo Christianus, or Philo's alleged conversion to Christianity, see D. R. Sills, "Re-Inventing the Past: Philo and the Historiography of Jewish Identity" (PhD diss., University of California at Santa

Barbara, 1984); and D. Runia, *Philo in Early Christian Literature: A Survey* (Minneapolis: Fortress, 1993).

15. For a brief survey of the evidence, see the discussions in A. Jacobs, *Remains of the Jews: The Holy Land and Christian Empire in Late Antiquity* (Stanford: Stanford University Press, 2004), 60–67; Lynn Cohick, "Jews and Christians," in The *Routledge Companion to Early Christian Thought*, ed. D. J. Bingham (London: Routledge, 2010), 79; and N. de Lange, *Origen and the Jews* (Cambridge: Cambridge University Press, 1976).

16. See the discussions in E. E. Urbach, "Homiletical Interpretations of the Sages and the Exposition of Origen on Canticles, and the Jewish-Christian Disputation," in *Studies in Aggadah and Folk-Literature*, ed. Y. Ben-Ami and Y. Dan (Jerusalem: Magnes Press, 1971), 247–279; R. Kimelman, "Rabbi Yochanan and Origen on the Song of Songs: A Third-Century Jewish-Christian Disputation," *Harvard Theological Review* 73, no. 3 (1980): 567–595. For further examinations of Origen's engagement with rabbis and their response to him, see also M. Niehoff, "Circumcision as a Marker of Identity: Philo, Origen and the Rabbis on Gen. 17.1–14," *Jewish Studies Quarterly* 20, no. 2 (2003): 89–123; and M. Himmelfarb, "The Ordeals of Abraham: Circumcision and the Aqedah in Origen, the Mekhilta and Genesis Rabbah," *Henoch* 30, no. 2 (2008): 289–310.

17. This book circulated in some Greek versions (Septuagint and Theodotion) of the Old Testament as a part of the canonical book of Daniel; it does not appear in any Hebrew versions and is not a part of the Jewish canon. On early debates over the status of Susanna and its use in Christian catacombs, see Susanna Drake, *Slandering the Jews: Sexuality and Difference in Early Christian Texts* (Philadelphia: University of Pennsylvania Press, 2013), 59–77.

18. Africanus, a Christian scholar, had questioned Origen's reference to the book as canonical in a public debate on the status of the book. Origen's reply cited his conversations with this unnamed Jewish expert: Origen, *Letter to Africanus*, 6.

19. It has been estimated that the entire work filled fifteen volumes and covered six thousand pages. Origen himself and his students later added two further columns. It has almost entirely disappeared, leaving only scattered

fragments from translations of some of its many versions. The original columns were the Hebrew text, the Hebrew text transliterated into Greek letters, followed by four Greek translations: Aquila, Symmachus, the Septuagint (LXX), and Theodotion.

20. Origen, *Letter to Africanus*, 5.

21. Origen, *Against Celsus*, 2.8.

22. There is a curious, even mysterious logic at work here, and Paul's language in Romans 11:33 admits as much: "O the depth of the riches and wisdom and knowledge of God! How unsearchable are his judgments and how inscrutable his ways!" It is worth noting, however, that in Paul's thinking this logic is thoroughly biblical. In Romans 10:19–21, he cites three biblical passages to justify his view of the special role of Gentiles in the divine plan of salvation: Deuteronomy 32:21; Isaiah 65:1; and Isaiah 65:2. Deuteronomy 32:21 reads: "I will make them [Israel] jealous with what is no people."

23. Jeremy Cohen, "The Mystery of Israel's Salvation: Romans 11:25–26 in Patristic and Medieval Exegesis," *Harvard Theological Review* 98, no. 3 (2005): 247–281. I will cite Origen's commentary from the translation in T. Scheck, *Origen: Commentary on the Epistle to the Romans* (Washington, D.C.: Catholic University of America Press, 2002). The text, with French translation, is now available in the Sources Chrétiennes (Paris: Editions du Cerf), vols. 532, 539, 543, and 555.

24. Cohen, "Mystery," 259.

25. Ibid., 260. In book 8.8, Origen states: "but when the fullness of the Gentiles enters in and Israel comes to salvation through faith in the end time" (Scheck, *Origen*, 170).

26. Cohen, "Mystery," 260.

27. Ibid., 263.

28. Ibid., 259.

29. On Jerome's work as a biblical scholar, see M. H. Williams, *The Monk and the Book: Jerome and the Making of Christian Scholarship* (Chicago: University of Chicago Press, 2006); see also Jacobs, *Remains of the Jews*, 67–100.

30. In his preface to the Vulgate translation of Job, Jerome singles out three of the Greek translations for criticism: those of Aquila the Jew, Symmachus,

and Theodotion the Judaizing (Christian) heretic, all of whom "buried the savior's mysteries under deceptive interpretations."

31. Jacobs, in *Remains of the Jews*, has argued that Jerome defended himself by turning his Jewish teachers into unwitting spokesmen for the truth of Christianity. In his treatment of Origen, Jerome, and Augustine, Jacobs uses the language of postcolonial writers to demonstrate the various techniques used by these ancient authors to colonize the Jews, to convert their Jewish knowledge into Christian truth, and to make them unwitting witnesses to the truth of Christianity. I have not used postcolonial theory, but we have arrived at similar conclusions.

32. Jerome lays out the issues in his letter 75; see the extended discussion in Jacobs, *Remains of the Jews*, 89–100.

33. Jerome, *Letter*, 112.12.

34. Augustine, *Letter*, 40.4.

35. See the game-changing book P. Fredriksen, *Augustine and the Jews: A Christian Defense of Jews and Judaism* (New York: Doubleday, 2010).

36. Cohen (in "Mystery") makes two important comments regarding differences between Origen, whose view may well have influenced Augustine, and the bishop of Hippo himself. First, "Augustine takes his explanation (for the fall and eventual restoration of the Jews) one step further than Origen's": "Not only did the fall of the Jews make room for the Gentiles . . . but the Jews' central role in spilling the salvific blood of Christ . . . specifically served God's purposes well" (274). But second, he adds that "Augustine's letter to Paulinus appears to have taken a step back from the Origenist position . . . 'All Israel' . . . evidently does not mean all Jews" (274–275).

37. R. M. Grant, *Gnosticism and Early Christianity* (New York: Columbia University Press, 1966), 141.

38. Wayne A. Meeks, *The Writings of St. Paul* (New York: Norton, 1972), 184.

1. WAS THE APOSTLE TO THE GENTILES THE FATHER OF CHRISTIAN ANTI-JUDAISM?

1. On Paul's impact in the early centuries of Christianity, see M. Wiles, *The Divine Apostle: The Interpretation of St. Paul's Epistles in the Early Church*

(London: Cambridge University Press, 1967); and A. Lindemann, *Paulus, Apostel und Lehrer der Kirche: Studien zu Paulus und zum frühen Paulusverständnis* (Tübingen: Mohr Siebeck, 1999).

2. The phrase is Tertullian's (*Against Marcion*, 3.5). He uses it ironically because he knew that Paul was popular among Christians whom Tertullian called heretics.

3. Gaston, *Paul and the Torah* (Vancouver: University of British Columbia Press, 1987), 15.

4. Robert G. Hamerton-Kelly, *Sacred Violence: Paul's Hermeneutic of the Cross* (Minneapolis: Fortress, 1992).

5. Heikki Räisänen, *Paul and the Law* (Tübingen: Mohr, 1987).

6. J. C. O'Neill, *Paul's Letter to the Romans* (Harmondsworth, UK: Penguin, 1975), 16.

7. J. C. O'Neill, *The Recovery of Paul's Letter to the Galatians* (London: Society for Promoting Christian Knowledge, 1972), 8.

8. I first laid out my views in *The Origins of Anti-Semitism: Attitudes Toward Judaism in Pagan and Christian Antiquity* (New York: Oxford University Press, 1983) and later revised and refined them in *Reinventing Paul* (New York: Oxford University Press, 2000).

9. Franz Mussner, *Tractate on the Jews* (Philadelphia: Fortress, 1984), 143.

10. Gaston, *Torah*, 92.

11. Stanley Stowers, *A Rereading of Romans: Justice, Jews, and Gentiles* (New Haven: Yale University Press, 1994), 129.

12. Paul Meyer, "Romans 10:4 and the 'End' of the Law," in *The Divine Helmsman: Studies on God's Control of Human Events, Presented to Lou H. Silberman*, ed. J. Crenshaw and S. Sandmel (New York: Ktav, 1980), 66.

13. Tertullian, *Against Marcion*, 5.2.

14. One interpreter of Ephesians has reimagined this document in line with, or better, in anticipation of, the view taken here: see Markus Barth, *Ephesians* (Garden City, N.Y.: Doubleday, 1974). Barth argues that the polemic of the letter is against Gentile Christian Judaizers, not against Jews (244–245), and that the position of the letter is that Gentiles are not required to become Jews, nor Jews to become Christians (310).

15. See D. Novak, *The Image of the Non-Jew in Judaism: The Idea of Noahide Law* (New York: E. Mellen Press, 2011).

16. So E. P. Sanders in his discussion of attitudes toward Gentiles among the early rabbis: see Sanders, *Paul and Palestinian Judaism: A Comparison of Patterns of Religion* (Philadelphia: Fortress, 1977), 207.

17. E. P. Sanders, *Jesus and Judaism* (Philadelphia: Fortress, 1985), 209.

18. See the discussion in T. Donaldson, *Paul and the Gentiles: Remapping the Apostle's Convictional World* (Minneapolis: Fortress, 1997), 60–74; and Donaldson, *Judaism and the Gentiles: Patterns of Universalism, to 135* CE (Waco, Tex.: Baylor University Press, 2007), 499–505. In the book published in 1997, Donaldson referred to Gentiles at the End as "eschatological pilgrims" (69), that is, Gentiles who repent and flock to Jerusalem but do not convert. Some of these texts include the following: Tobit 4:5–19; Micah 4:1; Isaiah 56:6–8; 66:20; 1 Enoch 90:30–38.

19. Paula Fredriksen, "Judaizing the Nations: The Ritual Demands of Paul's Gospel," *New Testament Studies* 56, no. 2 (2010): 242–243.

20. Krister Stendahl, *Paul Among Jews and Gentiles* (Philadelphia: Fortress, 1976).

21. Published in Gaston, *Paul and the Torah* (Vancouver: University of British Columbia Press, 1987), 15–34.

22. Stowers, *A Rereading of Romans*.

23. Gaston, personal communication.

24. Gaston, *Torah*, 15.

25. George Foot Moore, "Christian Writers on Judaism," *Harvard Theological Review* 14, no. 1 (1921): 197–254.

26. The published version of the lectures bears the title *The Political Theology of Paul* (Stanford: Stanford University Press, 2004).

27. The translators of the English edition confess that they modified some of Taubes's more intemperate language in the German original.

28. The sentence appears in a private letter by Taubes, cited in the editor's note (Taubes, *Political Theology*, 143). What Taubes had in mind in coining the word "Ahasueric" is a person, like Ahasuerus in the book of Esther, who is portrayed as unsteady and easily persuaded.

29. Ibid., 88.

30. Giorgio Agamben, *The Time That Remains: A Commentary on the Letter to the Romans* (Stanford: Stanford University Press, 2005); Alain Badiou, *Saint Paul: The Foundation of Universalism* (Stanford: Stanford University Press, 2003); Slavoj Žižek, "The Politics of Truth, or, Alain Badiou as a Reader of St Paul," in *The Ticklish Subject: The Absent Center of Political Ontology* (London: Verso, 1999).

31. Taubes, *Political Theology*, 3–4.

32. Ibid., 11.

33. Ibid., 24.

34. Ibid., 25.

35. Ibid., 47.

36. Ibid., 28 (his emphasis).

37. Ibid., 70.

38. D. Langton, *The Apostle Paul in the Jewish Imagination: A Study in Jewish-Christian Relations* (New York: Cambridge University Press, 2010), 252.

39. Ibid., 258.

40. See Gershom Scholem, *Sabbatai Sevi: The Mystical Messiah, 1626–1676* (London: Routledge and Kegan Paul, 1973). Sabbatai proclaimed himself to be the long-awaited Messiah and sparked an enthusiastic movement that stretched from western Europe to eastern Turkey. Many of his followers abandoned traditional Jewish practices, based on the belief that most Jewish practices would be canceled in the messianic age. In the end Sabbatai converted to Islam and brought consternation to his followers. Scholem, Taubes, and others were drawn to the obvious parallels between Sabbatai and Paul: alleged conversion to a new faith, abandonment of traditional Jewish practices, messianic claims, and so on.

41. Langton, *Apostle Paul*, 252.

42. Taubes, *Political Theology*, 20–21.

43. Ibid., 21 (his emphasis).

44. Ibid.

45. W. D. Davies, "Paul and the People of Israel," *New Testament Studies* 24, no. 1 (1977): 22.

46. Wayne A. Meeks, *Writings of St. Paul* (New York: Norton, 1972), 207.

47. W. Bauer, *Orthodoxy and Heresy in Earliest Christianity* (Philadelphia: Fortress, 1971), 227 (my emphasis).

48. Krister Stendahl, "The Apostle Paul and the Introspective Conscience of the West," *Harvard Theological Review* 56, no. 3 (1963): 199–215.

49. Ernst Käsemann, "Justification and Salvation History," in *Perspectives on Paul* (Philadelphia: Fortress, 1971), 62.

50. Heikki Räisänen, "Galatians 2.16 and Paul's Break with Judaism," *New Testament Studies* 31, no. 4 (1985): 543–553; and J. D. G. Dunn, *The Parting of the Ways Between Christianity and Judaism and Their Significance for the Character of Christianity* (London: SCM Press, 1991).

51. See S. Westerholm, *Perspectives Old and New: The "Lutheran" Paul and His Critics* (Grand Rapids, Mich.: Eerdmans, 2004). N. T. Wright, who has written widely on the subject, would probably place himself among the moderates; see Wright, *Paul and the Faithfulness of God* (Minneapolis: Fortress, 2013).

2. THE APOSTLE PAUL IN JEWISH EYES: HERETIC OR HERO?

1. Taubes, *Political Philosophy*, 5 (my emphasis).

2. Daniel Boyarin moves in a similar direction, viewing Paul as "an important Jewish thinker." Boyarin, *A Radical Jew: Paul and the Politics of Identity* (Berkeley: University of California Press, 1994), 2.

3. For surveys of Jewish approaches to Paul, see N. Fuchs-Kreimer, *The Essential Heresy: Paul's View of the Law According to Jewish Writers, 1886–1986* (PhD diss., Temple University, 1990); S. Meissner, *Die Heimholung des Ketzers: Studien zur jüdischen Auseinandersetzung mit Paulus* (Tübingen: Mohr Siebeck, 1996); and D. Langton, *The Apostle Paul in the Jewish Imagination: A Study in Jewish-Christian Relations* (New York: Cambridge University Press, 2010).

4. This punishment receives an extensive treatment in the Mishnah, tractate *Makkot*.

5. Heinrich Graetz, *History of the Jews* (Philadelphia: Jewish Publication Society, 1895), 5:680. Graetz's enemy was the nineteenth-century ex-Orthodox radical Reformer Samuel Holdheim. On Graetz, see I. Schorsch's

introduction to Graetz, *The Structure of Jewish History, and Other Essays* (New York: Jewish Theological Seminary of America, 1975).

6. Joseph Klausner, *Jesus to Paul* (New York: Macmillan, 1943), 534.

7. Ibid., 600 (my emphasis).

8. M. Bockmuehl, *Jewish Law in Gentile Churches: Halakhah and the Beginnings of Christian Public Ethics* (Edinburgh: T and T Clark, 2000), 172, who speaks in traditional terms of Paul's "ultimate undoing in Jewish eyes."

9. The phrase is in Richard Rubinstein, *My Brother Paul* (New York: Harper and Row, 1972), 114.

10. Martin Buber, *Two Types of Faith* (London: Routledge and Paul, 1951).

11. Ibid., 55.

12. See the discussion in Langton, *Apostle Paul*, 27–30.

13. The Karaite movement dates back to the ninth century CE, and defined itself against Rabbinic Judaism. Karaites rejected the authority of rabbis and of the massive postbiblical traditions preserved in Rabbinic texts (Mishnah, Talmuds, and numerous others). Karaites follow distinctive practices regarding Sabbath-observance and other practices. Small Karaite communities exist today in the United States, Turkey, and Israel. The Israeli scholar Daniel Lasker has written extensively on Karaism.

14. On Qirqisani, see L. Nemoy, "Al-Qirqisānī's Account of Jewish Sects and Christianity," *Hebrew Union College Annual* 7, no. 1 (1930): 317–397.

15. See L. Nemoy, "The Attitude of the Early Karaites Towards Christianity," in *Salo Wittmayer Baron Jubilee Volume*, vol. 2, ed. S. Lieberman (New York: Columbia University Press, 1974), 704.

16. Ibid., 372.

17. On Profiat Duran, see R. W. Emery, "New Light on Profiat Duran 'The Efodi,'" *Jewish Quarterly Review* 58, no. 4 (1968): 328–337; J. Cohen, "Profiat Duran's *The Reproach of the Gentiles* and the Development of Jewish Anti-Christian Polemic," in *Shlomo Simonsohn Jubilee Volume: Studies on the History of the Jews in the Middle Ages and Renaissance Period*, ed. D. Carpi (Tel Aviv: Tel Aviv University Press, 1992), 71–84; F. Talmage, "The Polemical Writings of Profiat Duran," in *Apples of Gold in Settings of Silver: Studies in Medieval Jewish Exegesis and Polemics*, ed. B. Walfish (Toronto: Pontifical Institute of Mediaeval Studies, 1999); and J. J. Schachter, "Rabbi

Jacob Emden, Sabbatianism, and Frankism: Attitudes Toward Christianity in the Eighteenth Century," in *New Perspectives on Jewish-Christian Relations: In Honor of David Berger*, ed. E. Carlebach and Schachter (Leiden: Brill, 2012), 359–396.

18. See the Hebrew edition by Frank Talmage, *The Polemical Writings of Profiat Duran: The Reproach of the Gentiles and "Be Not Like Unto Thy Fathers"* (Jerusalem: Merkaz Dinur, 1981). The only English translation was produced by Anne Deborah Berlin as an honors thesis at Harvard College (1987): "Shame of the Gentiles: A Fourteenth-Century Jewish Polemic Against Christianity." I will cite the relevant page numbers from Talmage and Berlin.

19. Talmage, *Polemical Writings*, 26–27; Berlin, *Shame*, 45. The distinguished Israeli historian Y. Baer states that Duran contrasts Paul's view of salvation with Judaism. But it is clear from the text that Duran is criticizing not Paul but medieval Christianity and its view of Paul. Baer, *A History of the Jews in Spain*, vol. 2 (Philadelphia: Jewish Publication Society of America, 1966), 152.

20. Talmage, *Polemical Writings*, 27; Berlin, *Shame*, 47.

21. Talmage, *Polemical Writings*, 29; Berlin, *Shame*, 46.

22. Talmage, *Polemical Writings*, 49; Berlin, *Shame*, 92.

23. Talmage, *Polemical Writings*, 23: Berlin, *Shame*, 38.

24. On Emden, see B. Greenberg, "Rabbi Jacob Emden: The Views of an Enlightened Traditionalist on Christianity," *Judaism* 27, no. 3 (1978): 351–363 and T. Willi, "Das Christentum im Lichte der Tora—Jakob Emdens Sendschreiben," in *Vergegenwärtigung des Alten Testaments . . . Festschrift für Rudolf Smend zum 70. Geburtstag*, ed. C. Bultmann, W. Dietrich, and C. Levin (Göttingen: Vandenhoeck und Ruprecht, 2002), 255–271.

25. For a detailed discussion of the *Toledot*, see chapter 5.

26. I have adapted the phrase from Daniel Stökl Ben Ezra, "An Ancient List of Christian Festivals in *Toledot Yeshu*: Polemics as Indication for Interaction," *Harvard Theological Review* 102, no. 4 (2009): 484. Stökl Ben Ezra's phrase is "a worldwide bestseller."

27. See the discussion in Sid Z. Leiman, "The Scroll of Fasts: The Ninth of Tebeth," *Jewish Quarterly Review* 74, no. 2 (1983): 174–195.

28. See Gager, "Simon Peter, Founder of Christianity or Saviour of Israel," in

Toledot Yeshu ("The Life Story of Jesus") Revisited, ed. Peter Schäfer, Michael Meerson, and Yaacov Deutsch (Tübingen: Mohr Siebeck, 2011), 226–245.

29. Luke 27:58 and parallels.

30. In the version known as *Tam u-Muad*, ed. G. Schlichting, *Ein jüdisches Leben Jesu: Die Verschollene Toledot-Jeschu-Fassung Tam ū-mū'ād* (Tübingen: Mohr Siebeck, 1982), 318ff.

31. S. Krauss, *Das Leben Jesu nach jüdischen Quellen* (Berlin: S. Calvary, 1902), 176.

32. The eleven volumes were published between 1853 and 1876. The first English translation appeared in 1891–1892.

33. Graetz, *Popular History of the Jews*, 2:158.

34. Klausner, *Jesus to Paul*, 534.

35. In his article on Paul in the *Encyclopaedia Judaica* 13 (1972): 190–191; on Flusser, see Gager, "Scholarship as Moral Vision: David Flusser on Jesus, Paul, and the Birth of Christianity," *Jewish Quarterly Review* 95, no. 1 (2005): 60–73.

36. Boyarin, *Radical Jew*, 22.

37. Graetz, *Popular History*, 2:153–155.

38. Ibid., 154. There is no text anywhere in Jewish literature, including Paul, that speaks of the entire Torah as being abrogated in the Messianic age, or at any other time. There is a small number of Rabbinic texts that speak of changes in the Law in the future. So, for example, *Vayikrah/Leviticus Rabbah* 9.7: "R. Phineas and R. Levi and R. Jonathan said in the name of R. Menahem of Galilee: 'In the time to come all sacrifices will be annulled, but that of Thanksgiving will not be annulled.'" These are to be dated well after Paul's time. The classic study remains W. D. Davies, *Torah in the Messianic Age and/or the Age to Come* (Philadelphia: Society of Biblical Literature, 1952).

39. Graetz, *Popular History*, 2:153.

40. Ibid.

41. Ibid., 155.

42. Ibid.

43. Ibid., 156.

44. Klausner, *Jesus to Paul*, 453.

45. Ibid.

46. Ibid., 453–454.

47. Buber, *Two Types of Faith*, 53–54 (my emphasis).

48. Ibid.

49. David Flusser, *Das Christentum—eine jüdische Religion* (Munich: Kösel-Verlag, 1990), 93.

50. Ibid.

51. Flusser, "Paul's Opponents in the Didache," in *Gilgul: Essays on Transformation, Revolution and Permanence in the History of Religions, dedicated to R. J. Zvi Werblowsky*, ed. S. Shaked, D. Shulman, and G. G. Stroumsa (Leiden: Brill, 1987), 33.

52. Boyarin, *Radical Jew*, 92. The theme of Paul's essential Jewishness runs through other Jewish readers. See, for instance, S. Ben-Chorin, *Paulus: Der Völkerapostel in jüdischer Sicht* (Munich: P. List, 1970): "there is scarcely any part of the massive structure of Pauline theology that is not Jewish" (181).

53. A physical description of Paul does appear in a later (mid-second century CE) Christian document, *Acts of Paul and Thecla*, 1.7. By that time Paul was long gone. The description is imaginary.

54. I owe the account of this anecdote to my friend and colleague Ora Limor.

55. See the account in C. Thoma, "David Flusser: Aussagen in Briefen und Vorträgen," *Freiburger Rundbrief* 2, no. 1 (2001): 86–93.

56. Pinchas Lapide and P. Stuhlmacher, *Paul: Rabbi and Apostle* (Minneapolis: Augsburg, 1984).

57. Ibid., 42.

58. Ibid., 48.

59. Ibid., 47.

60. See the full discussion in Langton, *Apostle Paul*, 211–219. The original Yiddish version has never been published.

61. Sholem Asch, *The Apostle* (New York: Putnam's, 1943), 21.

62. See Sholem Asch, *What I Believe* (New York: Putnam's, 1941): "He simply did not make circumcision a categoric condition for the gentiles who wanted to be received into the faith" (124).

63. Ibid., 517.

64. Ibid., 465 (my emphasis).

65. See Langton, *Apostle Paul*, 217–219. The criticism advanced by R. Gordis

remains firmly entrenched within old frameworks. Gordis, "Jesus, Paul and Sholem Asch," *Reconstructionist* 10, no. 5 (1944): 10–16. For a more balanced assessment, see N. Stahl, ed., *Sholem Asch Reconsidered* (New Haven: Beinecke Rare Book and Manuscript Library, 2004), the result of a Yale conference held in 2000.

66. Michael Wyschogrod, "The Law, Jews and Gentiles: A Jewish Perspective," *Lutheran Quarterly* 21, no. 4 (1969): 406.

67. Fuchs-Kreimer, *Essential Heresy*, cites several examples, among them Rubinstein, *My Brother Paul*.

68. Michael Wyschogrod, "The Dialogue with Christianity and My Self-Understanding as a Jew," in *Abraham's Promise: Judaism and Jewish-Christian Relations* (Grand Rapids, Mich.: Eerdmans, 2004), 231.

69. Lapide states the issue in almost identical terms. Speaking of the Christian view of Judaism as an arid religion of works righteousness, with Paul as the traditional source of this view, he comments: "Here a faithful Jew can only shake his head in bewilderment . . . all of this is an absurd caricature which finds its source in Paul" (37, 39).

70. Michael Wyschogrod, "A Jewish View of Christianity," in *Abraham's Promise*, 163.

71. Wyschogrod, "Dialogue," 234.

72. Lapide and Stuhlmacher, *Paul*, 42.

73. Wyschogrod, "Dialogue," 233.

74. I have decided not to include a discussion of the important Jewish philosopher Baruch/Benedict Spinoza (d. 1677). In his famous *Political-Theological Treatise*, Spinoza refers to Paul repeatedly as an example of a clear, rational, nonmagical thinker. This aspect of Spinoza's thought has received scant attention.

75. Pamela Eisenbaum, *Paul Was Not a Christian: The Real Message of a Misunderstood Apostle* (New York: HarperOne, 2009).

76. Mark Nanos, *The Mystery of Romans: The Jewish Context of Paul's Letter* (Minneapolis: Fortress, 1996); Nanos, *The Irony of Galatians: Paul's Letter in First-Century Context* (Minneapolis: Fortress, 2002).

3. LET'S MEET DOWNTOWN IN THE SYNAGOGUE: FOUR CASE STUDIES

1. In addition to the classic and still useful study of J. Juster, *Les Juifs dans l'empire romain: Leur condition juridique, économique et sociale* (Paris: P. Geuthner, 1914), see V. Tcherikover, *Hellenistic Civilization and the Jews* (Philadelphia: Jewish Publication Society of America, 1959); and E. Bikerman, *The Jews in the Greek Age* (Cambridge, Mass.: Harvard University Press, 1988). Important recent works include J. M. G. Barclay, *Jews in the Mediterranean Diaspora: From Alexander to Trajan, 323 BCE–117 CE* (Edinburgh: T and T Clark, 1996); J. J. Collins, *Between Athens and Jerusalem: Jewish Identity in the Hellenistic Diaspora* (Grand Rapids, Mich.: Eerdmans, 2000); and E. Gruen, *Diaspora: Jews Amidst Greeks and Romans* (Cambridge, Mass.: Harvard University Press, 2002).

2. Philo, *Embassy to Gaius*, 155–157.

3. Ibid., 156; Philo, *Life of Moses*, 2.215–216; Philo, *On Dreams*, 2.127.

4. Philo, *Gaius*, 132.

5. Tosefta, *Sukkah*, 4.6; also Jerusalem Talmud, *Sukkah*, 5.1, 55a–b; and Babylonian Talmud, *Sukkah*, 51b.

6. Philo, *On the Virtues*, 119.

7. Philo, *Gaius*, 245.

8. See E. Birnbaum, *The Place of Judaism in Philo's Though: Israel, Jews, and Proselytes* (Atlanta: Scholars Press, 1996), 193–219.

9. Philo, *On Rewards*, 152. Philo goes on to describe the unhappy fate of native Jews who prove unfaithful to their religion.

10. Philo, *Special Laws*, 52.

11. Erwin Goodenough, introduction to *Philo Judaeus* (Oxford: B. Blackwell, 1962), 30–45.

12. All of this is not to say that relations between Jews and non-Jews in Egypt were always amicable. They were not. As representatives of foreign conquerors, frequently in military roles, Jews were easy targets for indigenous Egyptian resentment of the ruling foreigners in Egypt (first the Persians,

then the Ptolemies, and finally the Romans). Whereas native Egyptians did not dare to confront these great powers directly, they could and did act out their resentments against their Jewish surrogates.

13. Philo, *Moses*, 2.17–24.

14. On other leading women in synagogues, see P. van der Horst, "Jews and Christians in Aphrodisias, in the Light of Their Relations on Other Cities of Asia Minor," *Nederlands Theologisch Tijdschrift* 43, no. 1 (1989): 106–121; reprinted in *Essays on the Jewish World of Early Christianity* (Göttingen: Vandenhoeck und Ruprecht, 1990), 166–181.

15. See B. Lifshitz, *Donateurs et fondateurs dans les synagogues juives* (Paris: J. Gabalda, 1967).

16. On women as leaders of synagogues, see B. Brooten, *Women Leaders in the Ancient Synagogue* (Chico, Calif.: Scholars Press, 1982).

17. Paul is imprisoned, flogged, or driven out of cities by civic authorities, sometimes in collaboration with Jews: Acts 13:50 (Antioch in Pisidia); 14:5 (Iconium); 14:19 (Lystra); 16:23 (Philippi); and 17:6 (Thessalonica).

18. It is put well in Martin Goodman, "The Persecution of Paul by Diaspora Jews," in *The Beginnings of Christianity*, ed. Jack Pastor and M. Mor (Jerusalem: Yad Ben-Zvi Press, 2005), 385: "The security of Jewish communities in Diaspora cities depended above all on Jews not interfering in the civic life, not least the religious civic life."

19. Goodman, "Persecution," 386, notes that "punishment was intended to prevent Paul from going round Diaspora cities incurring odium for local Jews from gentiles by urging those gentiles to cease their ancestral worship." The point is made explicitly in Acts 16:20–21: "When they brought them (Paul and Silas) before the local authorities, they (local pagans) said, 'These men are disturbing the city; they are Jews and are advocating customs that are not lawful for us as Romans to adopt or observe.'"

20. For a detailed and fully illustrated study of synagogue mosaics, especially in urban centers, see R. Hachlili, *Ancient Jewish Art and Archaeology in the Diaspora* (Leiden: Brill, 1998); and Erwin Goodenough, *Jewish Symbols in the Greco-Roman World* (New York: Pantheon, 1953–1968), passim.

21. Josephus, *Jewish Antiquities*, 20.3.

22. Horace, *Satires*, 1.4.142–143.

23. Dio Cassius, *History*, 57.18.5a.

24. See A. Linder, *The Jews in Roman Imperial Legislation* (Jerusalem: Israel Academy of Sciences and Humanities, 1987), 79–82, 124–132, 144–156, 256–262.

25. *Acts of Pionius*, 13.1.

26. S. Cohen concludes rather cautiously: "there may have been missionary trends among segments of Diaspora and Palestinian Jewry in the first century CE"; see S. J. D. Cohen, "Was Judaism in Antiquity a Missionary Religion," *Jewish Assimilation, Acculturation and Accommodation: Past Traditions, Current Issues and Future Prospects*, ed. M. Mor (Lanham, Md.: University Press of America, 1992), 20.

27. On John and his sermons, see W. A. Meeks and Robert Wilken, *Jews and Christians in Antioch in the First Four Centuries of the Common Era* (New York: Norton, 1978); and Robert Wilken, *John Chrysostom and the Jews: Rhetoric and Reality in the Late 4th Century* (Berkeley: University of California Press, 1983); see also I. Sandwell, *Religious Identity in Late Antiquity: Greeks, Jews, and Christians in Antioch* (Cambridge: Cambridge University Press, 2007).

28. Josephus, *Jewish War*, 7.45.

29. John Chrysostom, *Homilies*, 1.6.

30. Numerous synagogues from Late Antiquity included the phrase "this holy place" in their floor mosaics. A partial list includes synagogues from these sites: Stobi (in ancient Macedonia), Hammam Lif/Naro (near Tunis), Beth Shean (in modern Israel), Gaza, Hammat Tiberias (in modern Israel), Na'aran (near Jericho), and Alexandria.

31. Few Jews in the Diaspora knew Hebrew. They relied on Greek and Latin translations.

32. Pagan critics regularly mocked the lowly Greek of the Christian gospels; see J. G. Cook, *The Interpretation of the New Testament in Greco-Roman Paganism* (Tübingen: Mohr Siebeck, 2000).

33. On Gentile participation in various facets of Jewish life, see S. J. D. Cohen, "Crossing the Boundary and Becoming a Jew," in *The Beginnings of Jewishness: Boundaries, Varieties, Uncertainties* (Berkeley: University of California Press, 1999).

34. See the important article of S. J. D. Cohen, "Dancing, Clapping, Meditating: Jewish and Christian Observance of the Sabbath in Pseudo-Ignatius," in *Judaea-Palaestina, Babylon and Rome: Jews in Antiquity*, ed. B. Isaac and Y. Shahar (Tübingen: Mohr Siebeck, 2012), 29–53. John Chrysostom's remarks appear in his *On Lazarus* (*De Lazaro*); Augustine's in *His Expositions on the Psalms* (Psalm 32) and his *Treatise on the Gospel of John*, 3.19.

35. On the appeal of the Jewish Sabbath among Gentiles, see Robert Goldenberg, "The Jewish Sabbath in the Roman World," *Aufstieg und Niedergang der römischen Welt*, II, 19/1 (Berlin: De Gruyter, 1979), 414–447.

36. Mishnah, *Beitzah*, 5.2.

37. Babylonian Talmud, *Beitzah*, 30a.

38. John Chrysostom, *Homilies*, 1.

39. Cohen, "Dancing," 41.

40. Wilken, *John Chrysostom*, 161–162.

41. See page 147, note 3.

42. See the discussion by Sandwell, *Religious Identity*.

43. On Chrysostom's use of Paul, see M. Mitchell, *Heavenly Trumpet: John Chrysostom and the Art of Pauline Interpretation* (Tübingen: Mohr Siebeck, 2002).

44. See the major work of Joyce Reynolds and R. Tannenbaum, *Jews and God-Fearers at Aphrodisias: Greek Inscriptions with Commentary* (Cambridge: Cambridge Philological Society, 1987). For reassessments on important issues, see A. Chaniotis, "The Jews of Aphrodisias: New Evidence and Old Problems," *Scripta Classica Israelica* 21 (2002): 209–242.

45. As for the dates, Reynolds opts for the third century, while Chaniotis, "Jews of Aphrodisias," 213–218, argues for a much later date—fifth century for face a, fourth century for face b.

46. A marginal addition, running vertically to the left, reads: "Samouêl the elder of Perga."

47. Here it is worth noting that a number of the professions on the upper list deal with food and food preparation, suggesting that the Jews of Aphrodisias were concerned about Jewish food regulations. On the lower list, a number of professions point to building trades. Were these people

who had aided in the construction of the synagogue or some other Jewish building?

48. See the discussion in Reynolds and Tannenbaum, *Jews and God-Fearers*, 132, for evidence of ties between Jews and Blues elsewhere in Late Antiquity.

49. See Chaniotis, "Jews of Aphrodisias," 219–226; he adds a significant number of new finds uncovered subsequent to the publication of Reynolds and Tannenbaum, *Jews and God-Fearers*.

50. Van der Horst, "Jews and Christians," 108.

51. Chaniotis, "Jews of Aphrodisias," 231.

52. A. Chaniotis, "The Conversion of the Temple of Aphrodite at Aphrodisias," in *From Temple to Church: Destruction and Renewal of Local Cultic Topography in Late Antiquity*, ed. J. Hahn, S. Emmel, and U. Gotter (Leiden: Brill, 2008), notes signs of anti-Jewish sentiment at Aphrodisias in attempts to erase Jewish graffiti, perhaps in the sixth century (249).

53. Linder, *Legislation*, 74.

54. In his *Jewish Antiquities*, Josephus records a decree of Antiochus III to Zeuxis, governor of Lydia, ordering the transfer of two thousand Jewish families from Babylonia to Lydia and Phrygia. The decree does not mention Sardis, but the city lies in that region and was once the capital of the Lydian kingdom.

55. Josephus, *Antiquities*, 14.235–237, 260–263.

56. For the Greek inscriptions, see John Kroll, "The Greek Inscriptions of the Sardis Synagogue," *Harvard Theological Review* 94, no. 1 (2001): 5–55.

57. For the Hebrew inscriptions, see F. M. Cross, "The Hebrew Inscriptions from Sardis," *Harvard Theological Review* 95, no. 1 (2002): 3–19.

58. The literature on Sardis is enormous. See Lee I. Levine, *The Ancient Synagogue: The First Thousand Years* (New Haven: Yale University Press), 260–266. Kroll (see note 56) provides a full bibliography.

59. Marianne P. Bonz, "Differing Approaches to Religious Benefaction: The Late Third Century Acquisition of the Sardis Synagogue," *Harvard Theological Review* 86, no. 2 (1993): 139–154, along with many others.

60. Jodi Magness, "The Date of the Sardis Synagogue in Light of the Numismatic Evidence," *American Journal of Archaeology* 109, no. 3 (2005):

443–475. Magness's later dating is based on her discovery of coins under the floor, and thus in a sealed environment, dating from the late fifth and early sixth centuries. It is, of course, possible that the coins date only the floors and not the surrounding structures.

61. These six inscriptions were first published by the distinguished French epigrapher Louis Robert in *Nouvelles inscriptions de Sardes*, vol. 1 (Paris: Adrien Maisonneuve, 1964). Robert argued that *theosebês* in these inscriptions could not possibly refer to non-Jews; the term was too elevated, he wrote, and could only apply to pious Jews. Robert was wrong.

62. The numbers follow Kroll's publication.

63. Kroll, "Greek Inscriptions," describes *skutlôsis* as a "wall decoration of colored marble inlay" (11).

64. Clearly by this time, in the fourth, fifth, and sixth centuries, the somewhat looser terms in the Book of Acts had coalesced into the single, official term, *theosebês*. The term shows up in numerous Jewish inscriptions from all over the empire; see the full discussion in Reynolds and Tannenbaum, *Jews and God-Fearers*, 48–66.

65. Van der Horst, "Jews and Christians," 120.

66. On this multifaceted dynamic, see D. Satran, "Anti-Jewish Polemic in the Peri Pascha of Melito of Sardis: The Problem of Social Context," in *Contra Judaeos: Ancient and Medieval Polemics Between Christians and Jews*, ed. O. Limor and G. G. Stroumsa (Tübingen: Mohr Siebeck, 1996), 49–58.

67. See the original report, with exquisite detail, by C. Kraeling, *The Excavations at Dura Europos conducted by Yale University and the French Academy of Inscriptions and Letters: Final Report VIII*, part 1, *The Synagogue*, ed. A. R. Bellinger, F. E. Brown, A. Perkins, and C. B. Welles (New Haven: Yale University Press, 1979). See also, Goodenough, *Jewish Symbols*, vol. 9; Hachlili, *Ancient Jewish Art*, 96–197; and K. Weitzmann and H. L. Kessler, *The Frescoes of the Dura Synagogue and Christian Art* (Washington, D.C.: Dumbarton Oaks, 1990).

68. Levine, *Ancient Synagogue*, 253.

69. I estimate that by including the missing panels on the two side walls and the obliterated east wall, the total number of panels could be as high as forty-five.

70. In the rubble fill from the main street leading to the synagogue complex, a piece of parchment turned up with a fragmentary Hebrew text.

71. Samuel also shows up in two Greek inscriptions (nos. 23–24); Abram appears in one (no. 25).

72. See the discussion by B. Geiger, "The Middle Iranian Texts," in Kraeling, *Excavations*, 283–318.

73. D. MacDonald, "Dating the Fall of Dura-Europus," *Historia* 35, no. 1 (1986) has suggested that these visitors might have been "Iranian Jews, who are known to have absorbed much of Persian culture even to the extent of adopting Iranian names, or Persians deeply interested in the Jewish religion, the Iranian equivalent of 'God-Fearers' in the Roman Empire, or both" (62).

74. Geiger, "Middle Iranian," 314.

75. Not everyone was delighted by what they saw. The eyes of several figures in the frescoes have been gouged. Kraeling, *Excavations*, 338, assigned the gouging to Roman soldiers. Goodenough, *Jewish Symbols*, 9:23, attributed the work to a disgruntled Jew. C. P. Kelley, after examining the location of the gouges, comes down on Kraeling's side; see Kelley, "Who Did the Iconoclasm in the Dura Synagogue," *Bulletin of the American Schools of Oriental Research* 295 (1994): 57–72.

76. See the discussion in Kelley, "Iconoclasm," 57–58.

77. K. B. Stern, "Tagging Sacred Space in the Dura-Europos Synagogue," *Journal of Roman Archaeology* 25, no. 1 (2012): 171–194.

78. Ibid., 188.

79. Ibid. Stern cites an Aramaic graffito from a nearby town that specifically curses passersby who look at a remembrance-inscription and fail to recite it: "the curse of [Marna] against anyone who reads this inscription [and does not say, 'Remembered'] for good be so-and-so."

80. See Levine, *Ancient Synagogue*, 255–256; and Hachlili, *Ancient Jewish Art*, 180–182.

81. On the frequent representation of the Jerusalem Temple in Jewish (and Christian) structures in Late Antiquity, see R. Talgam, "The Representations of the Temple in Jewish and Christian Houses of Prayer in the Holy Land in Late Antiquity," in *Jews and Christians*, 222–248.

82. Kessler, *Frescoes*, 179.

83. Claude Lévi-Strauss, *The Raw and the Cooked* (New York: Harper and Row, 1969), 16.

84. See K. Stern, "Mapping Devotion in Roman Dura Europos: A Reconsideration of the Synagogue Ceiling," *American Journal of Archaeology* 114, no. 3 (2010): 473–504. In the article, Stern has drawn attention to the 234 surviving ceiling tiles—the original number may have been closer to 450. Various aspects of the ceiling lead her to emphasize the ritual role of the ceiling in the overall space of the sanctuary: its role "in demarcating a space as appropriate for devotion of prayer" (497); its function to distinguish a "three-dimensional sacred structure from the mundane world outside" (498); and the interplay of frescoes and ceiling in demarcating "the synagogue as a sacred space" (501). Her language that the murals of the synagogue "transported viewers to distant biblical lands and times" is strikingly similar to my own, without having influenced it directly. This is a case of happy coincidence.

85. The theme of the temple's revival runs throughout much of Jewish art in Late Antiquity; it is especially prominent in the synagogue at Sepphoris; see Z. Weiss, *Promise and Redemption: A Synagogue Mosaic from Sepphoris* (Jerusalem: Israel Museum, 1996).

86. Leonard Rutgers, *Making Myths: Jews in Early Christian Identity Formation* (Leuven: Peeters, 2009), 104–105.

87. Fredriksen, "Post-Roman West," 255.

88. See the discussion in J. H. A. Wijnhoven, "The Zohar and the Proselyte," in *Readings on Conversion to Judaism*, ed. L. Epstein (New York: Scribner's, 1995), 47–49.

89. Martin Goodman, "Proselytising in Rabbinic Judaism," in Epstein, *Readings*, 34–35; see also B. Z. Wacholder, "Attitudes Toward Proselytizing in the Classical Halakah," in Epstein, *Readings*, 15–32.

4. TWO STORIES OF HOW
EARLY CHRISTIANITY CAME TO BE

1. Harnack, *What Is Christianity?* (New York: Harper, 1901), 190.

2. Sanders, *Paul and Palestinian Judaism: A Comparison of Patterns of Religion* (Philadelphia: Fortress, 1977), 551.

3. Here I follow Lloyd Gaston, "Anti-Judaism and the Passion Narrative in Luke and Acts," in *Anti-Judaism in Early Christianity*, vol. 1, ed. P. Richardson with D. Granskou (Waterloo, Ont.: Wilfred Laurier University Press, 1986), 127–153.

4. On the strikingly negative image of Peter in Mark, see John Gager, "Simon Peter, Founder of Christianity or Saviour of Israel," in *Toledot Yeshu ("The Life Story of Jesus") Revisited*, ed. Peter Schäfer, Michael Meerson, and Yaacov Deutsch (Tübingen: Mohr Siebeck, 2011), 221–246.

5. See G. P. Luttikhuizen, as quoted by M. de Boer, "The Nazoreans: Living at the Boundary of Judaism and Christianity," in *Tolerance and Intolerance in Early Judaism and Christianity*, ed. G. N. Stanton and G. G. Stroumsa (New York: Cambridge University Press, 1998), who prefers the name "early Christian Judaism" for the Nazoreans and other similar groups (241). See also A. Y. Reed, " 'Jewish Christianity' After the 'Parting of the Ways,' " in *The Ways That Never Parted*, ed. A. Becker and A. Y. Reed (Tübingen: Mohr Siebeck, 2003), 189–231. This volume has sparked lively responses, not all of them supportive; see M. H. Williams, "No More Clever Titles: Observations on Some Recent Studies of Jewish-Christian Relations in the Roman World," *Jewish Quarterly Review* 99, no. 1 (2009): 37–55.

6. The Greek word *christos* is used over forty times in the Greek Old Testament (Septuagint) where it translates the Hebrew word *maschiach*. The English word *messiah* is a rough transliteration of *maschiach* as it passed, untranslated, through Greek and Latin to modern Western languages. In John 1:41, Andrew, speaking of Jesus, reports to his brother Peter, "We have found the *messias*." And the text adds, "which is translated as *christos*." Again in 4:25, the woman at the well says to Jesus, "I know that the *messias* is coming." And again the editor adds, "Who is called *christos*."

7. Moshe Weinfeld, "The Charge of Hypocrisy in Matthew 23 and in Jewish Sources," *Immanuel* 24/25 (1990): 52–58. The Babylonian Talmud, *Sotah*, 22b, speaks of the seven types of Pharisees, five of which are portrayed in a negative light. This passage comes as a commentary on a saying of R. Joshua, in Mishnah, *Sotah*, 3.4, which speaks of various forms of hypocritical piety, among them the "self-inflicted wounds of the Pharisees," all of which "ruin the world."

8. Tosefta, *Hagiga*, 2.1.

9. Weinfeld, "Charge of Hypocrisy," 57.

10. Ibid., 58.

11. Anthony J. Saldarini, *Matthew's Christian-Jewish Community* (Chicago: University of Chicago Press, 1994), 7.

12. Ibid., 22. Even Saldarini is probably too conservative in dating the emergence of a clear Christian identity to the second century. A much later date now seems preferable.

13. Ibid., 193.

14. See Moore, "Christian Writers on Judaism," 197–254.

15. Ibid., 197.

16. Sanders, *Palestinian Judaism*.

17. Charlotte Klein, *Anti-Judaism in Christian Theology* (Philadelphia: Fortress, 1978).

18. Saldarini, *Matthew's Christian-Jewish Community*, 205: "The gospel's polemics have been used again and again by gentile Christians as a club to beat the whole Jewish tradition, marginalizing the Jewish community and threatening its existence."

19. Many modern interpreters regard the final sentence ("And thus he declared . . . ") as a later interpolation that both misunderstands and distorts the meaning of the first sentence ("There is nothing . . . ").

20. Yair Furstenberg, "Defilement Penetrating the Body: A New Understanding of Contamination in Mark 7.15," *New Testament Studies* 54, no. 2 (2008): 178; so also D. Boyarin, *The Jewish Gospels: The Story of the Jewish Christ* (New York: New Press, 2012), 104, following Furstenberg.

21. Menachem Kister, "Plucking on the Sabbath and Christian-Jewish Polemic," *Immanuel* 24/25 (1990), 35–51; Kister, " 'Leave the Dead to Bury Their Own Dead,' " in *Studies in Ancient Midrash*, ed. James L. Kugel (Cambridge: Harvard University Center for Jewish Studies, 2001), 43–56; and Kister, "Law, Morality, and Rhetoric in Some Sayings of Jesus," in Kugel, *Studies*, 145–154.

22. Kister, "Law," 151–152.

23. Kister, "Plucking on the Sabbath," 35.

24. In his brief commentary to the gospel of Mark, Daniel Stökl Ben Ezra writes that "Mark is a Jewish gospel written for readers who were familiar

with Jewish traditions and institutions"; see Stökl Ben Ezra, "Markus-Evangelium," *Reallexicon für Antike und Christentum* 24 (2010): column 186.

25. Boyarin, *Jewish Gospels*, 127.

26. See the brief discussion in C. E. Evans, "The New Testament Canon," in *The Cambridge History of the Bible from the Beginnings to Jerome*, ed. P. R. Ackroyd and C. E. Evans, vol. 1 (Cambridge: Cambridge University Press, 1970), 280–282.

27. David Frankfurter, "Jews or Not," *Harvard Theological Review* 94, no. 4 (2001): 416.

28. Ibid., 415: "In Jewish texts of the early Roman period, *zenut* [the Hebrew equivalent of *porneia*] often refers to intermarriage between Jews and Gentiles"; see also Christine Hayes, "Intermarriage and Impurity in Ancient Jewish Sources," *Harvard Theological Review* 91, no. 1 (1999): 3–36.

29. Elaine Pagels, *Revelations: Visions, Prophecy, and Politics in the Book of Revelation* (New York: Viking, 2012), notes that the Greek term *parthenos* "does not mean that these men [and women?] never had sexual intercourse, but rather that they were practicing sexual abstinence to keep themselves pure . . . for holy war" (50).

30. See the comment by Pagels: "Those whom John says Jesus 'hates' look very much like Gentile followers of Jesus converted through Paul's teaching" (ibid., 54, her emphasis).

31. John Marshall, *Parables of War: Reading John's Jewish Apocalpse* (Waterloo, Ont.: Wilfred Laurier University Press, 2001).

32. For general surveys of these groups, see A. F. J. Klijn and G. I. Reinink, *Patristic Evidence for Jewish-Christian Sects* (Leiden: Brill, 1973); and J. Carleton Paget, "Jewish Christianity," in *The Cambridge of Judaism*, vol. 3, *The Early Roman Period*, ed. W. Horbury, W. D. Davies, and J. Sturdy (Cambridge: Cambridge University Press, 1999), 731–775.

33. Epiphanius, *Panarion*, 30.16.8–9.

34. Ibid., 30.16.6. The Greek is *praxeis apostolón*, the title of the Book of Acts in the New Testament in early manuscripts.

35. Andrew S. Jacobs, *Christ Circumcised: A Study in Early Christian History and Difference* (Philadelphia: University of Pennsylvania Press, 2012), 103.

36. On the Nazoreans, see de Boer, "The Nazoreans."

37. Jerome, *Epistle*, 112.13.

38. P. Vielhauer, "Jewish-Christian Gospels," in *New Testament Apocrypha*, vol. 1 (Philadelphia: Westminster Press, 1963), 146.

39. Among his many works on this subject, see F. Stanley Jones, *An Ancient Jewish Christian Source on the History of Christianity: Pseudo-Clementine "Recognitions" 1.27–71* (Atlanta: Scholars Press, 1995).

40. Reed, " 'Jewish Christianity,' " 207 (my emphasis). So also F. Stanley Jones, "An Ancient Jewish Christian Rejoinder to Luke's Acts of the Apostles," in *The Apocryphal Acts of the Apostles in Intertextual Perspective*, ed. R. Stoops (Atlanta: Scholars Press, 1997), 223–245.

41. Pseudo-Clementines, *Recognitions*, 1.43, 50.

42. Shlomo Pines, "The Jewish Christians of the Early Centuries of Christianity According to a New Source," in *Proceedings of the Israel Academy of Sciences and Humanities*, vol. 2 (Jerusalem: Central Press, 1968), 237–309; republished in *The Collected Works of Shlomo Pines*, ed. G. G. Stroumsa, vol. 4 (Jerusalem: Magnes Press, 1996), 237–286. My references will be to the republished version.

43. S. M. Stern, "Abd al-Jabbar's Account of How Christ's Religion Was Falsified by the Adoption of Roman Customs," *Journal of Theological Studies* 19, no. 1 (1968): 128–185.

44. See G. G. Stroumsa, "Jewish Christianity and Islamic Origins," in *Islamic Cultures, Islamic Contexts: Essays in Honor of Patricia Crone*, ed. B. Sadeghi, A. Q. Ahmed, R. Hoyland, and A. Silverstein (Leiden: Brill, 2014), 72–96. In his wide-ranging essay on the historiography of Jewish Christianity, Stroumsa argues that some Jewish-Christian groups survived into the seventh century CE.

45. Patricia Crone, "Islam, Judeo-Christianity and Byzantine Iconoclasm," *Jerusalem Studies in Arabic and Islam* 2, no. 1 (1980): 59–95.

46. Ibid., 74.

47. Ibid., 86.

48. The Roman satirist, writing in the first half of the second century CE, writes of a Roman father, clearly a Judaizer, who honors the Jewish Sabbath (*metuentum sabbata*) but whose son goes on to become a full convert; see the

discussion in M. Stern, *Greek and Latin Authors on Jews and Judaism*, vol. 2 (Jerusalem: Israel Academy of Sciences and Humanities, 1980), 103–107. The second half of Epictetus's saying (see the following note) goes on to speak of full converts: "But when he adopts the attitude of mind of the man who has been baptized and has made his choice, then he is a Jew in fact and is also called one."

49. The Stoic philosopher Epictetus (from the first half of the second century) quotes what must have been a widespread saying: "Whenever we see someone hesitating between two faiths we are in the habit of saying, 'He is not a Jew but is only acting the part.' " The passage from Epictetus is cited by Arrian, *Dissertationes*, 2.9.19–21.

50. For a full survey of the evidence, see John Gager, *The Origins of Anti-Semitism* (New York: Oxford University Press, 1983), 59–61.

51. From Seneca, *On Superstition*, as quoted by Augustine, *City of God*, 6.11.

52. Acts refers to these Judaizers as fearers (*phoboumenoi*: 13.16, 26) and worshipers (*sebomenoi*: 16.14; 18.7) of God. At a later date, as we will see, the common and official term to designate Judaizers will become *theosebês*.

53. Josephus, *Against Apion*, 2.282.

54. Philo, *Moses*, 2.17.

55. Ibid., 2.41–42.

56. Ignatius, *Magnesians*, 10.

57. See the discussion in James Parkes, *The Conflict of the Church and the Synagogue* (New York: Atheneum, 1961), 174–177.

58. On Aphrahat and the Jews, see J. Neusner, *Aphrahat and Judaism: The Christian-Jewish Argument in Fourth- Century Iran* (Atlanta: Scholars Press, 1999); and N. Koltun-Fromm, "A Jewish-Christian Conversation in Fourth-Century Persian Mesopotamia," *Journal of Jewish Studies* 47, no. 1 (1996), 45–63.

59. Neusner, *Aphrahat*, 4.

60. Koltun-Fromm, "Jewish-Christian Conversation," 51–53.

61. Aphrahat, *Demonstrations*, 21.1.

62. Samuel Krauss, "The Jews," *Jewish Quarterly Review* 6, no. 1 (1893): 88–89. Krauss published a series of four articles under this title between 1892 and

1894. These articles have now been republished in a single volume, *The Jews in the Works of the Church Fathers: Sources for Understanding the Aggadah* (Piscataway, N.J.: Gorgias Press, 2007).

63. So also Neusner, *Aphrahat*, 5.

64. Here I follow the distinction drawn by G. Langmuir, *Toward a Definition of Antisemitism* (Oakland: University of California Press, 1990). For Langmuir, what differentiates anti-Semitism from anti-Judaism is the emergence of irrational fantasies and beliefs about Jews; Langmuir also calls them "chimerical assertions." Langmuir dates these fantasies, beliefs, and assertions to the twelfth century. But by his own definition, I believe that John Chrysostom and Ephrem must be described as anti-Semites. Shepardson does not use the term "anti-Semitism," but it is not too much to suggest that her use of "vitriolic" (22, 31, 34) to describe Ephrem's language brings us close to anti-Semitism.

65. Christine Shepardson, *Anti-Judaism and Christian Orthodoxy: Ephrem's Hymns in Fourth-Century Syria* (Washington, D.C.: Catholic University of America Press, 2008).

66. Kathleen McVey, *Ephrem the Syrian: Hymns* (New York: Paulist Press, 1989); and McVey, "The Anti-Judaic Polemic of Ephrem Syrus' Hymns on the Nativity," in *Of Scribes and Scrolls: Studies on the Hebrew Bible, Intertestamental Judaism, and Christian Origins*, ed. H. W. Attridge, J. J. Collins, and T. H. Tobin (Lanham, Md.: University Press of America, 1990), 229–240.

67. Shepardson, *Anti-Judaism*, 34.

68. Ibid., 43.

69. Krauss, "The Jews," 91.

70. See D. Levenson, "The Ancient and Medieval Sources for the Emperor Julian's Attempt to Rebuild the Jerusalem Temple," *Journal for the Study of Judaism* 35, no. 4 (2004): 409–460.

71. Krauss, "The Jews," 93–99.

72. McVey, *Ephrem the Syrian*, 238. In his important essay "Date and Provenance of the Aramaic *Toledot Yeshu*," in Schäfer, Meerson, and Deutsch, *Revisited*, 13–26, Michael Sokoloff argues that the Aramaic *Toledot* probably originated in Jewish Babylonia toward the middle of the first millennium

CE. In other words, the right place and time for Ephrem. His home town, Nisibis, was an important center of Rabbinic Judaism.

73. This incident sent shock waves as far as Milan. The emperor Theodosius I had ordered the bishop in Callinicum to rebuild the synagogue at his own expense. Ambrose, the bishop of Milan, wrote to Theodosius (letter 40) ordering him to rescind his ruling. His language in the letter is outrageous—the synagogue is a place of perfidy and impiety; all synagogues should be destroyed; the bishop's own laziness had prevented him from burning down the synagogue in Milan; see Gager, *Origins of Anti-Semitism*, 120; and Drake, *Slandering the Jews*, 102.

74. For lists of sites where synagogues were destroyed or transformed into churches, see J. Juster, *Les Juifs dans l'empire romain: Leur condition juridique, économique et sociale*, vol. 1 (Paris: P. Geuthner, 1914), 464–469; M. Simon, *Verus Israel: A Study of the Relations Between Christians and Jews in the Roman Empire, 135–425* (New York: Oxford University Press, 1986), 265–266; S. Fine, "The Menorah and the Cross: Historiographical Reflections on a Recent Discovery from Laodicea on Lycus," in *New Perspectives on Jewish-Christian Relations: In Honor of David Berger*, ed. E. Carlebach and J. J. Schachter (Leiden: Brill, 2012), 34.

75. A law of Theodosius (*Cod. Theod.* 16.8.9), dated to 393, specifically prohibits the destruction of synagogues and states that no law declares Judaism to be illegal.

76. Fergus Millar, "Christian Emperors, Christian Church and the Jews of the Diaspora in the Greek East, CE 379–450," *Journal of Jewish Studies* 55, no. 1 (2004): 1–24.

77. Ibid., 7.

78. Ibid., 3.

79. Born in Hungary as Tunde Szentes, she took the name of Marie after her mother Emma received baptism; Emma spent much of the war period as a rescuer of Jews, working frequently with Raoul Wallenberg. See the somewhat hagiographic account of Emma's life by Ramon Sender Barayon, "Mother Myriam and Emma Szentes: A Nun Discovers Her Jewish Mother" (1986), www.raysender.com/myrian.html.

80. Epiphanius, *Heresies*, 7.1; 9.1.

81. The words of an anonymous reviewer of my manuscript. Her/his emphasis.

82. See G. Strecker, "On the Problem of Jewish Christianity," appendix to *Orthodoxy and Heresy in Earliest Christianity*, by W. Bauer (Philadelphia: Fortress, 1971), 285.

83. Paula Fredriksen, "Roman Christianity and the Post-Roman West: The Social Correlates of the Contra Iudaeos Tradition," in *Jews, Christians and the Roman Empire*, ed. N. B. Dohrmann and A. Y. Reed (Philadelphia: University of Pennsylvania Press, 2013), 257: "Conditions varied depending on the locale and on the temperament of the particular bishop."

84. Joan Taylor, "The Phenomenon of Jewish-Christianity: Reality or Scholarly Invention?," *Vigiliae Christianae* 44, no. 4 (1990): 327.

85. Becker and Reed, *The Ways That Never Parted*.

86. It should be noted that virtually all of the evidence cited here comes from outside Palestine: Steven Fine, "Non-Jews in the Synagogues of Late-Antique Palestine: Rabbinic and Archeological Evidence," in *Jews, Christians, and Polytheists in the Ancient Synagogue*, ed. Steven Fine (New York: Routledge, 1999). While it is true that "no synagogue inscription from Palestine reflects the presence of proselytes or God-fearers in Palestinian synagogues" (230), there is literary evidence that non-Jews made donations to synagogues (226–230). One such text is Acts 10, not cited by Fine, where a Roman centurion (a senior military officer) of the Italian Cohort is described as "a devout man, who feared God with all his household and gave alms generously to the [Jewish] people and prayed constantly to God." Cornelius was clearly a god-fearer and an active participant in a local Palestinian synagogue.

87. See Crone, "Islam," 91.

88. See the discussion in A. Linder, *Legislation*, 80–82 and passim.

89. *Cod. Theod.*, 1.7.1.

90. Ibid., 16.7.3.

91. Ibid., 3.7.2 and 9.7.5.

92. Fredriksen, "Post-Roman West," 258.

93. Ibid., 263.

94. Agobard's views are expressed in two writings, *De Judaicis superstitionibus*

and *De insolentia Judaeorum*; see the discussion in Schäfer, "Agobard's and Amulo's *Toledot Yeshu*, in Schäfer, Meerson, and Deutsch, *Revisited*, 27–48.

95. Leonard Rutgers, "Archaeological Evidence for the Interaction of Jews and Non-Jews in Late Antiquity," *American Journal of Archaeology* 96, no. 1 (1992): 113.

5. TURNING THE WORLD UPSIDE DOWN: AN ANCIENT JEWISH LIFE OF JESUS

1. See the brief discussion in Deutsch, "The Second Life of the Life of Jesus," in *Toledot Yeshu ("The Life Story of Jesus") Revisited*, ed. Peter Schäfer, Michael Meerson, and Yaacov Deutsch (Tübingen: Mohr Siebeck, 2011, 289–290; see also R. Chazan, *Daggers of Faith: Thirteenth Century Christian Missionizing and Jewish Response* (Berkeley: University of California Press, 1989), 115–136.

2. Y. Deutsch has noted a puzzling gap in witnesses to the *Toledot* between the time of Amulo and the early part of the thirteenth century: Deutsch, "Second Life," 287. The thirteenth century also marks the first Jewish witnesses to the *Toledot*. On the reception of the *Toledot*, see Deutsch, "Second Life," 281–295; S. Krauss, *Leben Jesu nach jüdischen Quellen* (Berlin: S. Calvary, 1902), 2–23; and W. Horbury, *A Critical Examination of the Toledot Jeshu* (PhD diss., Cambridge University, 1970).

3. See the discussion in M. Radin, "A Papal Brief of Pius IV," *Jewish Quarterly Review* 1, no. 1 (1910): 113–121.

4. See *Toledot Yeshu*: *Toledot Yeshu: The Life Story of Jesus*, edited and translated by Michael Meerson and Peter Schäfer, in collaboration with Yaacov Deutsch, David Grossberg, Avigail Manekin, and Adina Yoffe, vol. 1, *Introduction and Translation*, vol. 2, *Critical Edition* (Tübingen: Mohr Siebeck, 2014). The editors describe the publications as follows: "Currently, we finished transcribing more than one hundred manuscripts in Hebrew and Aramaic and have developed a sophisticated database that allows us to compare different versions and variant readings of *Toledot Yeshu*. Using the database, we translated the representative manuscripts and supplemented

their texts with a critical apparatus and brief commentaries. The final product of our work will combine a critical and synoptic edition of select *Toledot Yeshu* manuscripts, their translation, and, in addition, an electronic database of all available Hebrew and Aramaic manuscripts of *Toledot Yeshu.*"

5. See Krauss, *Leben Jesu.*

6. Horbury, *A Critical Examination.*

7. Riccardo di Segni, *Il Vangelo del Ghetto* (Rome: Newton Compton, 1985).

8. On biblical and philosophical criticism of Christianity, see D. Berger, *Jewish-Christian Debate in the High Middle Ages: A Critical Edition of the Niẓẓaḥon Vetus with an Introduction, Translation, and Commentary* (Philadelphia: Jewish Publication Society of America, 1979); D. Lasker, *Jewish Philosophical Polemics Against Christianity in the Middle Ages* (New York: Ktav, 1977).

9. Other fragments were discovered in the nearby Karaite synagogue.

10. See the important article by Miriam Goldstein, "Early Jewish-Christian Polemic in Arabic: Judeo-Arabic Versions of *Toledot Yeshu,*" *Ginzei Qedem* 6, no. 1 (2012): 9–42.

11. For Luther's Latin source and his German translation, *Vom Schem Hamphoras und vom Geschlecht Christi,* see B. Callsen, F. P. Knapp, M. Niesner, and M. Przybilski, eds., *Das jüdische Leben Jesu Toldot Jeschu: Das älteste lateinische Übersetzung in den Falsitates Judeorum von Thomas Ebendorfer* (Vienna: Oldenbourg, 2003), 97–106.

12. On Voltaire's use of the *Toledot,* see D. Barbu, "Voltaire and the Toledot Yeshu: A Response to Philip Alexander," in *Infancy Gospels: Stories and Identities,* ed. C. Clivaz, A. Detwiler, L. Devillers, and E. Norelli (Tübingen: Mohr Siebeck, 2011), 617–627.

13. On Huldreich, see A. Yoffie, "Observations on the Huldreich Manuscripts of the *Toledot Yeshu,*" in Schäfer, Meerson, and Deutsch, *Revisited,* 27–48, 61–77.

14. See the discussion in Horbury, *A Critical Examination,* 1–23.

15. On Celsus and his Jewish sources, see M. Niehoff, "A Jewish Critique of Christianity from Second-Century Alexandria: Revisiting the Jews in Contra Celsum," *Journal of Early Christian Studies* 21, no. 2 (2013): 151–175.

16. Tertullian, *On Spectacles*, 30.5–6. Of this passage, S. Krauss wrote that Tertullian already knew at this early date "den ganzen Inhalt" (the entire contents) of the *Toledot* (*Leben Jesu*, 3).

17. On the discovery of the Geniza (treasure-room) of the Cairo synagogue, see A. Hoffman and P. Cole, *Sacred Trash: The Lost and Found World of the Cairo Geniza* (New York: Schocken, 2011).

18. In the Aramaic version translated by H. Basser in *The Frank Talmage Memorial Volume*, vol. 1, ed. B. Walfish (Haifa: Haifa University Press, 1993), 277.

19. Notably the Strasbourg version (Krauss, *Leben Jesu*, 45), which contains other traces of influence from Aramaic versions), and the late version known as Tam u-Muad.

20. Number 81 in the Mosseri collection; in the Cambridge University collection it is listed as T-S ns 329.820.

21. See the full discussion by Peter Schäfer, "Agobard's and Amulo's *Toledot Yeshu*," in Schäfer, Meerson, and Deutsch, *Revisited*, 27–48.

22. The verb in Luke 2:47, *existanto*, normally translated with the positive sense of "admiration," need not carry that meaning. It might just as well be taken to mean something like "they were dumbfounded, confused, stunned."

23. No such event occurs in the New Testament gospels, but it does appear in the various versions of infancy gospels; see S. Davis, "Bird Watching," in *Christ Child: Cultural Memories of a Young Jesus* (New Haven: Yale University Press, 2014), 47–63.

24. In his article "Christian Origins in Jewish Tradition," *New Testament Studies* 13, no. 4 (1967), E. Bammel has suggested that the gospel of John (7:45–53) may point to an earlier examination of Jesus before the Jewish authorities (326): "So the chief priests and the Pharisees called a meeting of the council."

25. In other versions Judas ejaculates on Jesus, while in some late medieval versions Judas sodomizes him. See the discussion by R. Karras, "The Aerial Battle in the *Toledot Yeshu* and Sodomy in the Late Middle Ages," *Medieval Encounters* 19, no. 5 (2013): 493–533.

26. Chapter 1 of the gospel of John narrates Jesus's choice of five disciples: two in 1:35, one named Andrew, the other anonymous; one in 1:42, Peter, called Andrew's brother; one, Philip, in 1:43; and one, Nathanael, in 1:45. Five

is also the number of disciples in the trial-story of Jesus's disciples in the Babylonian Talmud, *Sanhedrin*, 43a–b. Their names are: Matthai, Nakai, Netzer, Buni, and Todah. The story revolves around a series of swapped proof-texts exchanged between the sages and the disciples; the disciples cite a text in their favor, the sages respond with one against them. This passage, using these same names, shows up in both Aramaic and Hebrew versions of the *Toledot*. See the full discussion in P. Schäfer, *Jesus in the Talmud* (Princeton: Princeton University Press, 2007), 75–81.

27. See Yassif, "Toledot Yeshu: Folk-Narrative and Self-Criticism," in Schäfer, Meerson, and Deutsch, *Revisited*, 101–135.

28. Ibid., 132.

29. Ibid., 133. M. Sokoloff's linguistic analysis of the Aramaic fragments points in the same geographical direction, though to a somewhat earlier date. He describes the provenance of the Aramaic *Toledot* as "Jewish Babylonia . . . towards the middle of the first millennium CE," in Sokoloff, "The Date and Provenance of the Aramaic *Toledot Yeshu* on the Basis of Aramaic Dialectology," in Schäfer, Meerson, and Deutsch, *Revisited*, 25.

30. Yacov Deutsch, "New Evidence of Early Versions of *Toledot Yeshu*," *Tarbiz* 69 (2000): 177–197.

31. Deutsch comments that there exist many parallels between the underlying Aramaic of the Firkovich and the Aramaic fragments but that there are sufficient differences to conclude that the Aramaic source of the Firkovich was not identical to the versions revealed in the extant fragments; Ibid., 180–181.

32. There is reason to believe that the phrase "from the holy spirit" may be a later addition to the original story, designed to clear up any ambiguity as to who had impregnated Mary.

33. Morton Smith, *Jesus the Magician* (New York: Harper and Row, 1978), 47.

34. It would appear that the additional phrase *ek tou nekrou* (from the dead) was added to an earlier version of the story to eliminate any ambiguity.

35. On the burial stories in the *Toledot*, see the important article H. Newman, "The Death of Jesus in the *Toledot Yeshu* Literature," *Journal of Theological Studies* 50, no. 1 (1999): 59–79.

36. See the discussion in S. Z. Leiman, "The Scroll of Fasts: The Ninth of Te-beth," *Jewish Quarterly Review* 64, no. 2 (1983): 174–195.

37. Krauss, *Leben Jesu*, 47–48 and 61–62.

38. Ibid., 85 and 113–114. Clearly certain traits are transferred from Peter stories to Paul, or vice versa.

39. Tam u-Muad, *Ein jüdisches Leben Jesu: Die Verschollene Toledot-Jeschu-Fassung Tam ū-mū'ād*, ed. G. Schlichting (Tübingen: Mohr Siebeck, 1982), paragraph 330.

40. Krauss, *Leben Jesu*, 176–177. On connections between Elijah and John, see Matthew 16:14 and John 1:21.

41. See P. S. van Koningsveld, "The Islamic Image of Paul and the Origins of the Gospel of Barnabas," *Jerusalem Studies in Arabic and Islam* 20 (1996): 210; see also Stern, "Abd al-Jabbar's Account," 177–181. The tradition began before ibn Ḥazam and lasted long after him.

42. For a discussion of these host-desecration charges, see M. Rubin, *Gentile Tales: The Narrative Assault on the Medieval Jew* (New Haven: Yale University Press, 1999).

43. Ebendorfer mentions a Jewish convert (*quodam Hebreo fidelissimo*) who had aided him in making the translation; see Przybilski, *Das jüdische Leben Jesu Toldot Jeschu*, 39.

44. The marginal gloss reads, *xera australica* (anti-Jewish decrees); see Przybilski, *Das jüdische Leben Jesu Toldot Jeschu*, 27.

45. On injunctions in other *Toledot* manuscripts to keep them secret, see Deutsch, "Second Life," 283–284.

46. Przybilski, *Das jüdische Leben Jesu Toldot Jeschu*, 37. On the late-medieval practice of reading the *Toledot* on Christmas Eve, see M. Shapiro, "Torah Study on Christmas Eve," *Journal of Jewish Thought and Philosophy* 2 (1999): 319–353.

47. See Przybilski, *Das jüdische Leben Jesu Toldot Jeschu*, 25–26, and the literature cited there. It should be noted here that the first author to study the pogrom was Samuel Krauss, *Die Wiener Geserah vom Jahre 1421* (Vienna: W. Braunmüller, 1920).

48. See Krauss, *Leben Jesu*, 165–172.

49. This theme is treated at length in P. Schäfer, *Jesus in the Talmud*; and I. Yuval, *Two Nations in Your Womb: Perceptions of Jews and Christians in Late Antiquity and the Middle Ages* (Berkeley: University of California Press, 2006).

50. There is a considerable body of literature on Jewish conversions to Christianity in the Middle Ages: see J. Cohen, *The Friars and the Jews: The Evolution of Medieval Anti-Judaism* (Ithaca: Cornell University Press, 1982); D. Berger, "Mission to the Jews and Jewish-Christian Contacts in the Polemical Literature of the High Middle Ages," *American Historical Review* 91 (1986): 576–591; and Chazan, *Daggers*.

51. In his article "Jewish Converts to Christianity in Medieval Europe, 1200–1500," in *Cross Cultural Convergences: Essay Presented to Aryeh Grabois on His Sixty-Fifth Birthday*, ed. M. Goodich, S. Menache, and S. Schein (New York: P. Lang, 1995), J. Shatzmiller holds that not all conversions led to bitter separations, even between spouses. He provides a useful survey of Jewish conversions and their various motivations across Europe (and England).

52. See Paola Tartakoff, "The *Toledot Yeshu* and Jewish-Christian Conflict in the Medieval Crown of Aragon," in Schäfer, Meerson, and Deutsch, *Revisited*, 297–309. Using official documents from the Spanish Inquisition, Tartakoff recounts the story of a Jew who converted to Christianity but subsequently returned to Judaism after hearing stories from the *Toledot*. He later returned to Christianity again; as a reward for his return, he was sentenced to life in prison.

53. B. Heller, "Über das Alter der jüdischen Judas-Sage und das Toldot Jeschu," *Monatsschrift für Geschichte und Wissenschaft des Judentums* 77 (1933): 208. The translation is from Newman, "The Death of Jesus," 59 (my emphasis).

6. EPILOGUE

1. Sanders, *Paul and Palestinian Judaism: A Comparison of Patterns of Religion* (Philadelphia: Fortress, 1977), 4.

2. Ibid., 35.

3. Stanley Stowers, *A Rereading of Romans: Justice, Jews, and Gentiles* (New Haven: Yale University Press, 1994), 327.

4. Ibid.

5. Gaston, personal communication

6. See chapter 5.

7. S. Meissner, *Die Heimholung des Ketzers: Studien zur jüdischen Ausein-andersetzung mit Paulus* (Tübingen: Mohr, 1996).

8. Michael Wyschogrod, "Incarnation," *Pro Ecclesia* 2, no. 2 (1993): 215.

9. Ibid. (my emphasis).

10. Pinchas Lapide and P. Stuhlmacher, *Paul: Rabbi and Apostle* (Minneapolis: Augsburg, 1984), 42.

11. Michael Wyschogrod, *Abraham's Promise: Judaism and Jewish-Christian Relations* (Grand Rapids, Mich.: Eerdmans, 2004), 236.

12. I first laid out my views in *The Origins of Anti-Semitism in Pagan and Christian Antiquity* (New York: Oxford University Press, 1983) and later revised and refined them in *Reinventing Paul* (New York: Oxford University Press, 2000).

13. Review by R. Goldenberg in *Religious Studies Review* 11, no. 4 (1985): 337.

14. Of course, some evangelicals hold that at the End, Jews must accept Jesus Christ to be saved. Others hold that Jews do not need to convert at all, that they are redeemed by the divine covenants with Abraham and Moses.

INDEX

Abba Shaul/Paul, 44, 134
Abner of Burgos, 138
Acts of Pionius, 62
Africanus, Julius, 149n18
Against All Heretics (Epiphanius), 100
Against Celsus (Origen), 121–122
Against Heresies (Irenaeus), 99–101
Against the Jews (Tertullian), 148n12
Agobard, 115, 117, 124
Albrecht, VI, Duke of Austria, 135
al-Jabbar, Abd, 101, 104–105
Amulo, 124
Ananias, 62
anti-Israel set, Pauline texts, 19
anti-Judaism, Christian: Christian
    elites on, 113; development of,
    58; Ephrem and, 109–111; Jewish
    response to, 131, 137, 139, 144–145;
    Kessler on, 84; language of, 85;
    Lapide and, 48; literary forms of,
    4–6; Luke on, 90; Matthew and,
95; passed from words to deeds,
    110–111; Paul as father of, 14, 18–
    19, 21–23, 28–30, 39, 97, 140–141;
    Rutgers on, 85; Wyschogrod as
    chief source and spokesman of, 49,
    51, 143
Antioch (present-day Turkey), 62–66,
    110–111
Antiochus III, 63, 165n54
Antiochus IV Epiphanes, 63
anti-Pauline leaders, within Jesus-
    movement, 26–27
anti-Semitism: Ephrem and, 109–111;
    Jews and, 139; Lapide and, 48;
    modern, 145; passed from words to
    deeds, 110–111; source of, 30; threat
    to Jewish communities of, 137
Aphrahat, 107–109; representing clas-
    sic case of Christian anti-Judaism,
    109
Aphrodisias, 66–70, 67*f*, 68*f*

Apocalypse of John. *See* Book of
   Revelations
The Apostle (Asch), 48–49
"The Apostle Paul and the Introspec-
   tive Conscience of the West"
   (Stendahl), 34–35
Aramaic fragments, 180n31
Aramaic graffiti, 167n79
Aramaic, *Toledot Yeshu* in, 123–124,
   174–175n72
archisynagogoi (leaders of the syna-
   gogue), 100
Asch, Sholem, 48–49, 142
Asia Minor, 54, 59, 90, 92, 100
Augenspiegel, of Reuchlin, 118
Augustine of Hippo, 7, 10–13, 12, 24,
   64, 100, 143

Babylon, 53–54
Babylonian Talmud, 53–54, 64
Baer, Y., 157n19
Becker, A., 113
Berlin, Anne Deborah, 157n18
Beroea, 59
birth stories, of Jesus: in Celsus,
   121–122; in Matthew, 128–130; in
   Toledot Yeshu, 119, 124, 129–130
bishops: Agobard, 85, 115, 117, 124;
   Ambrose, 175n73; Amulo, 117, 124;
   anti-Judaism of, 112; Augustine
   of Hippo, 10; church-building of,
   114–115; decrees issued by, 107;
   destruction of synagogues by, 110;
   role of, 4
Book of Acts, 38–39, 41, 58–66, 89, 92,
   104, 106, 166n64

Book of Revelations, 97–98
Boyarin, Daniel, 45, 47, 96, 142, 155n2
Buber, Martin, 40, 45, 46, 48, 142

Carthage, 148n12
Cassius, Dio, 62
Celsus, 121–122, 129
Chorin, Ben, 142
Christiani, Pablo, 138
"Christian Emperors, Christian
   Church and the Jews of the
   Diaspora in the Greek East, CE
   379–450" (Millar), 111
Christianity/Christians: antiquity and
   authenticity of, 6–7; Christian tri-
   umphalism, 7; conflict and tension
   between Jews and, 3–5, 147–148n8;
   early Christianity, stories of how
   it came to be, 87–115; Eastern
   Christianity, 107; embrace of by
   Constantine, 2; leaders, distinc-
   tive role of, 4; at Magnesia, 107; at
   Sardis, 74
Chrysostom, John, 6, 62, 64, 65–66,
   85, 107, 109
circumcision, 19, 25–26, 98
Codex Theodosianus, 114, 175n75
Cohen, Jeremy, 9, 151n36
Cohen, Shaye, 65
"commandments of God," in Book of
   Revelation, 97
"conceptual nihilation," 147n7
Constantine, 1–2
conversions, 38, 138, 171–172n48,
   182n50
Corinth, 59

Cornelius, 61
Crone, Patricia, 105
Cronica Austrie (Ebendorfer), 136
Cyrus, 53

Daniel, canonical book of, 149n17
Davies, W. D., 34
debates, in *Toledot Yeshu*, 125
dekania, 69
Demonstrations (Aphrahat), 107–109
Deutsch, Yaacov, 118, 127, 177–178n4,
    177n2, 180n31
"devout converts" (*sebomenoi prosêlu-*
    toi), 59–60
di Segni, Riccardo, 118
Dialogue with Trypho (Martyr), 99,
    120–121, 148n13
Diaspora, Jews in the, 1–2
Diaspora synagogues, 61–62
do Valladolid, Alfonso, 138
Donin, Nicholas, 138
Dura Europos, 75–84, 76*f*, 77*f*, 78*f*
Duran, Profiat: on Paul, 41–45,
    142–143

early Christianity, stories of how it
    came to be, 87–115
Eastern Christianity, 107
Eben Bohan [Touchstone] (ibn Shap-
    rut), 124
Ebendorfer, Thomas, 135–136
Ebionites, 99–101
Edict of Toleration, 70
Egypt, Jewish Diaspora in, 54–55
Eisenbaum, Pamela, 51, 142
Elephantine (Yeb), 55

Eliahu / Elijah. *See* Paul
Eliezer, R., 29
Emden, Jacob, 41–45, 43, 142, 143
Ephesians, 152n14
Ephrem, 107–110
Epictetus, 172n49
Epiphanius, 100, 112–113
Epistle of Barnabas, 28
Eybeschütz, Jonathan, 42

Firkovich, Abraham, 127, 180n31
Flusser, David, 45, 46–47, 51, 142
The Forward (newspaper), 49
Frankfurter, David, 97–98
Fredriksen, Paula, 29, 114–115
Furstenberg, Yair, 95, 142

Gager, John G., 143
Galerius, 70
Gaston, Lloyd, 18, 22, 29–30, 141, 144
Gentile proselytes, 28
god-fearers (*theosebês*), 29, 60–61
Goodenough, Erwin, 57
Goodman, M., 85
Graetz, Heinrich: on Paul, 39, 142; on
    Paul's primary concern of bringing
    salvation to Gentiles, 45–46
Grant, Robert, 13
Greek translation, of Hebrew Bible, 55
Grossberg, David, 177–178n4

Hamerton-Kelly, Robert, 21
hand-washing practices, of Pharisees,
    95
Harnack, Adolf von, 6–7, 13, 18, 88
hebraica veritas, 10

Hebrew version, of *Toledot Yeshu*,
123–124
Heliopolis, temple at, 55
heresiologists, 98–101, 105, 112–113
Hexapla, 7–8
History of the Jews (Graetz), 45–46
Horbury, William, 118
Huldreich, Johann, 120
Hymns of the Nativity (Ephrem), 110

ibn Marwan, Daud, 40
ibn Shaprut, 124
Iconium, 59
Ignatius, 2–4, 107
Irenaeus, 99–101
Italy, Jewish settlements in, 54

Jacobs, Andrew, 100–101, 151n31
James, 25, 89, 92, 102
James, letter of, 13
Jeremiah, 54–55
Jerome, 7, 9–12, 150–151n30
Jerusalem Temple, 167n81
Jerusalem Post (newspaper), 111
Jesus: ancient Jewish life of (see *Toledot Yeshu* [*The Life of Jesus*]);
birth of in *Toledot Yeshu*, 128–132;
body of in *Toledot Yeshu*, 126;
burial in *Toledot Yeshu*, 128–132;
choice of five disciples by, 179–
180n26; compared with Paul, 42;
crucifixion of in *Toledot Yeshu*,
126; education of in *Toledot Yeshu*,
124–125; as first founder of Christianity, 87–88; fleeing of in *Toledot
Yeshu*, 125; power of in *Toledot*

Yeshu, 125; struggle with Judas in
Toledot Yeshu, 125–126; threat of to
Judean leaders, 5
Jesus-movement, anti-Pauline leaders
within, 26–27
Jewish Christianity, 101–106, 113
Jewish Diaspora, 53–58
Jewish Sabbath, 5, 42, 54, 56, 61,
64–65, 88, 99–100, 111, 133–134,
171–172n48
Jews: in the Diaspora, 1–2, 143;
Origen on, 7–9; Paul as a, 31–33,
41, 144; Paul's engagement with,
37–38; protected during Cru-
sades, 148n10; relations between
Christians and, 3–5, 147–148n8;
relations between non-Jews and,
161–162n12
"The Jews in the Works of the Church
Fathers" (Krauss), 108–109
Joel, prophet, 54
John: as author of Book of Revela-
tions, 97–98; as a disciple of Jesus,
89; gospel of, 63–65, 124–126,
128–130
John Paul II, Pope, 144
John the Baptist, 43, 119, 123, 130, 134
Josephus, 62, 63, 70, 106–107, 165n54
Joshua, R., 29
Judaism: Christian view of, 159n69;
distorted view of, 141; evidence
for the appeal of, 106; Philo of
Alexandria on, 56–57; social and
political status of, 1–2; women at-
tracted to, 61
judaizing, Christian, 11–12, 85, 106–113

judaizing, pagan, 106–107
Julian, 110
Justin Martyr, 99, 114, 120–121, 148n13

Karaite movement, 156n13
Käsemann, Ernst, 34–35
Kefa, Shimon. *See* Peter
Kessler, Herbert, 84
Kister, Menachem, 96, 142
Klausner, Joseph, 39, 45, 46, 47, 142
Klein, Charlotte, 95, 140, 141
Krauss, Samuel, 108–110, 118, 134,
    178n16, 181n47

Langmuir, G., 174n64
Lapide, Pinchas, 48, 51, 142, 159n69
Letter to Africanus (Origen), 8
Lévi-Strauss, Claude, 84
Life of Moses (Philo of Alexandria),
    107
Louis the Pious, 85, 115
Luke, gospel of, 90, 93, 98, 128–129,
    131
Luther, Martin, 120
Luttikhuizen, G. P., 91

makkot, punishment, 155n4
Manekin, Avigail, 177–178n4
Marcion, 13, 14
Mark, gospel of, 13, 44, 87, 91, 95–96,
    124–126, 128, 131, 144
Marti, Ramon, 117
Mary Catherine, Sister, 111–112
Matthew, gospel of, 93, 117, 128–129,
    131
McVey, Kathleen, 109–110

Meeks, Wayne, 13
Meerson, Michael, 177–178n4
Meissner, Stefan, 142
Melito of Sardis, 74
Millar, Fergus, 111
miracles, in *Toledot Yeshu*, 125
missions, 14, 45–46, 51, 56, 61–62,
    103
Moore, G. F., 30–31, 95, 140, 141
Mosaic Law (*halakhah*), 11, 48, 93, 95,
    99, 100, 103, 114
Myriam, Mother, 114

Nanos, Mark, 51, 142
Nazoreans, 99–101
Nebuchadnezzar, 53, 54
Neusner, Jacob, 108
New Testament: counternarratives in,
    91–98; counternarratives outside
    the, 98–101
new view of Paul: conclusions of,
    33–35; what's wrong with, 28–31
Nierenberg, David, 147–148n8
Noachide commandments (*mishpatei
    ha-torah*), 28–29, 43
Nostra Aetate, 144
Nouvelles inscriptions de Sardes (Rob-
    ert), 166n61

Obadiah, 54
On the Contemplative Life (Philo), 98
On Unleavened Bread (Ephrem), 109
O'Neill, J. C., 21
Onias IV, 55
Origen, 7–10, 13, 100, 121–122, 136,
    149–150n19

The Origins of Anti-Semitism: Attitudes Toward Judaism in Pagan and Christian Antiquity (Gager), 143

Pandera, Joseph, 124, 129
Panthera, 122, 129
parthenos, 171n29
Paschal/Easter Homily (Melito), 74
Paul: about, 17–18; on arguments against validity of circumcision and Mosaic covenant, 27; arrived in Rome as a prisoner, 54; Asch on transformation of, 48–49; Augustine on, 12; in Book of Acts, 89, 103; compared with Jesus, 42; concern for Gentile believers of, 27, 45–46; conversion in life of, 38, 89; dispute between Peter and, 11, 13; engagement with Jews of, 37–38; as father of Christian anti-Judaism, 14, 18–19; as a Jew, 31–33, 41, 144; in Jewish eyes, 37–52; language of in Romans, 150n22; in modern Jewish readers, 45–51; Origen's treatment of, 8–9; rejection-replacement, 14; as second founder of Christianity, 88; in synagogues, 59–61; threefold Jewish view of, 39; in *Toledot Yeshu*, 43, 133–134
Paul Among Jews and Gentiles (Stendahl), 29–30
"Paul and the Torah" (Gaston), 29–30
Perga, 59
Persian / Achaemenid empire, 53

Peter: as an observant Jew, 41; conversion in life of, 89; dispute between Paul and, 11, 13; in gospel of Mark, 44; in *Toledot Yeshu*, 43–44, 133–134
2 Peter, 13
Petronius, Roman governor, 57
Pharisees, 5, 25, 62, 93–95, 125, 131, 169n7
Philippi, 59
Philo of Alexandria: 54–57, 98, 107, 148–149n14
Pines, Shlomo, 104–105
Pius VI, 118
Pogrom in Vienna, 135–136
Political-Theological Treatise (Spinoza), 160n74
pro-Israel set, in Pauline letters, 19–20
proselytes, 28, 57, 60, 79–80, 84–85, 100, 106, 176n86
Pseudo-Clementines, 28, 101–105
pseudoconversions, 138
Ptolemies, 55, 161n12
Pugio Fidei [*Dagger of Faith*] (Marti), 117

Qirqisani, 40

Rabbinic Judaism, 40
Räisänen, Heikki, 21
Recognitions (Reed), 102–103
Reed, Annette Yoshiko, 91, 102–103, 113
Remains of the Jews (Jacobs), 151n31
A Rereading of Romans: Justice, Jews, and Gentiles (Stowers), 30

resigned technique, for resolving tensions between Paul's letters, 21

Reuchlin, Johannes, 118

"rhetorical" Jews, 6

"righteous Gentiles," 28–29

Robert, Louis, 166n61

Rome, Jewish settlements in, 54

Rosen-Zvi, Ishay, 142

Rufinus, 10, 12

Rutgers, Leonard, 85, 115

Sabbatai Zvi, 154n40

Sabbath, 5, 42, 54, 56, 61, 64–65, 88, 99–100, 111, 133–134, 171–172n48

Saldarini, Anthony, 94

Sanders, E. P., 29, 34, 95, 140–141

Sardis, 70–74, 71*f*, 72*f*, 73*f*

Saul. *See* Paul

Schäfer, Peter, 177–178n4

Scholem, Gershom, 33

Seneca, 1, 106

Sepharad, 54

settings: statements about Law and circumcision, 26; in which Paul write his letters, 24–25

Severa, Julia, 61

The Shame (Kelimat) of the Gentiles (Duran), 41

Shepardson, Christine, 109

Siebeck, Mohr, 177–178n4

Simon, Marcel, 6–7

Sokoloff, Michael, 142, 174–175n72, 180n29

Soloveitchik, Joseph, 49

Song of Songs, 7

Spinoza, Benedict, 142, 160n74

standard tale, of how early Christianity came about, 87–91, 112–113

Stendahl, Krister, 22, 29–30, 34–35, 38

Stern, Karen, 81, 167n79, 168n84

Stern, Samuel, 104–105

Stowers, Stanley, 30, 141

Strasbourg manuscript, of *Toledot Yeshu*, 134

subordination technique, for resolving tensions between Paul's letters, 21

supersession, Christian, 11–12

synagogues: *archisynagogoi* (leaders of the synagogue), 100; conclusions about, 84–85; destruction of, 110–111, 175n74; Diaspora, 61–62; floor mosaics in, 163n30; Gentiles and, 58–85; leading women in, 162n14; Paul in, 59–61; transformation of, 175n74

Szentes, Tunde, 175n79

Tam u-Muad manuscript, of *Toledot Yeshu*, 134, 179n19

Taubes, Jacob, 31–33, 37, 142, 153n28

Taylor, Joan, 112–113

Tertullian, 13, 24, 100, 122–123, 148n12, 152n2

Theodosius I, 1, 2, 175n73

theosebês, 60, 66–67, 73–74, 166n64, 173n52

Thessalonica, 59

"those who fear or revere God" (*phoboumenoi ton theon*), 59–60

Toledot Yeshu [*The Life of Jesus*]: about, 14, 41–45; in Aramaic, 123–124, 174–175n72; basic facts about,

Toledot Yeshu [*The Life of Jesus*] (continued)
119–123; conclusions from, 136–138; deceiving believers in, 103; Deutsch on, 177n2; early version of, 110; hybrid version of, 127–128; Jesus's birth in, 128–132; Jesus's burial in, 128–132; part 2 of, 133–135; Peter in, 43–44; Pines on, 105; Pogrom in Vienna and, 135–136; reason for neglect of, 118; Siebeck on, 177–178n4; translated into Latin, 135–136; versions of, 123–124
Torah, 19, 23, 25–26, 39, 41–43, 51, 75–76, 93, 96–97, 102, 143, 158n38
Tosefta, 29, 56
Toward a Definition of Antisemitism (Langmuir), 174n64
The True Word (Celsus), 121–122
Trypho, 99, 148n13

Valentinus, 13, 14
Vielhauer, Philipp, 101
Vienna manuscript, of *Toledot Yeshu*, 134

Voltaire, 118, 120
Vulgate Bible, 10

Wagenseil, Johan, 120
Wallenberg, Raoul, 175n79
The Ways That Never Parted: Jews and Christians in Late Antiquity and the Early Middle Ages (Becker and Reed), 113
Weinfeld, Moshe, 94
Wiener Gesera, 136
Wilken, Robert, 65
women: attracted to Judaism, 61; in synagogues, 162n14
"worshipers of God" (*sebomenoi theon*), 59–60
Wyschogrod, Michael, 49–51, 142–143, 144

Yassif, Eli, 126–127, 141
Yochanan, 129–130
Yoffe, Adina, 177–178n4

zenut, 171n28